THE INTELLIGENT GUIDE TO

TEXAS HOLD'EM POKER

Sam Braids

Intelligent Games Publishing
Towson, Maryland

The Intelligent Guide to Texas Hold'em Poker
Copyright © 2003 by Intelligent Games Publishing

Book cover writing by Susan Kendrick Writing

Intelligent Games Publishing
P. O. Box 6705, Towson, MD 21285
Web Site: www.intelligentpoker.com
E-mail: comments@intelligentpoker.com
Write the publisher for bulk price quotes.

ISBN·0-9677551-2-3
Library of Congress Control Number: 2003100272

Publisher's Cataloging-in-Publication
(Provided by Quality Books, Inc.)

Braids, Sam.
   The intelligent guide to Texas hold'em poker / Sam
Braids.
   p. cm.
   Includes bibliographical references and index.
   LCCN 2003100272
   ISBN 0967755123

   1. Poker. 2. Gambling.   I. Title.

GV1251.B73 2003   795.41'2
                             QBI03-200081

PLEASE NOTE: The material contained in this book is for informational purposes only. In no manner should this book be construed to offer legal advice on the issue of online gambling. It is the reader's responsibility to know and follow the laws that apply in his or her state and jurisdiction. Seek appropriate legal advice from a qualified attorney if unsure. The publisher does not endorse or guarantee any of the services described in this book. The reader assumes all risks and responsibility for his or her actions. If you do not agree with these conditions, you may return this book to the publisher for a full refund.

CONTENTS

LIST OF FIGURES AND TABLES

PREFACE

This book is a concise guide to the rapidly expanding world of Texas Hold'em Poker. It provides an overview, vocabulary, and concepts that are essential to the play of Texas Hold'em, and to reading and interpreting the complex literature on the game. My motivation is to provide a guide to Texas Hold'em that informs readers without overwhelming them.

For the beginner: This book will teach the rules of Hold'em poker, conduct in both public cardrooms and online poker games, the fundamental tactics and strategies for play, and point you towards further resources, both in print and online.

For the experienced player: This book is meant to provide a framework for thinking about Hold'em poker and serve as a reference. Carefully planned tables, charts, graphs, illustrations, and strategic summaries are provided to efficiently assist players in their real-time poker decisions. With the growth of online poker in recent years, it is possible for players to have charts and tables in front of them while they play. Some of these charts were designed with that use in mind.

Some features unique to this book are:

- A discussion of online poker that includes how to set up to play online, the differences between online and in-person poker (Chapter 3), and where to go for online poker (Chapter 10).

- A strategy section that explains how to adjust your play to different game conditions. Successful poker players use a dynamic approach, constantly fine-tuning their play to prevailing game conditions. Included is a game observation form for online Hold'em that is used to focus your strategic thinking before you enter a game (Chapter 6).

- A section with essays on mathematical and psychological considerations necessary for success. A series of stories are told that illustrate key concepts in action. These vignettes, mostly real-life examples, should aid the reader in putting into practice all the principles and information contained in this book (Chapters 7–8).

- Reviews of books and web sites. Do you want to know about other books on poker, purchase poker products, or locate a cardroom nearest your home or place where you plan to travel? You will find all of this information (Chapters 9–10).

- A quick explanation of common Hold'em variants such as Omaha and Pineapple, (Appendix I) and Poker Tournaments (Appendix II).

Texas Hold'em poker is a complex and subtle game. Simply following a set of instructions will not make you a successful player. Mastering the game requires hours of both study and practice, and a commitment to a long-term, disciplined approach to play. This book is a road map to use on your journey.

Sam Braids
February 2003

Introduction

This book provides a concise summary of Texas Hold'em poker, including rules, conduct, tactics, and strategies. Read this book to:

- Learn the rules of Texas Hold'em.
- Learn poker terminology.
- Learn to play Texas Hold'em in a public cardroom.
- Learn to play Texas Hold'em online.
- Learn the fundamental tactics and strategies.
- Learn to become a winning poker player.

The goal of this book is to provide the tools you need to play an intelligent game of Texas Hold'em in any venue, and to give you a greater understanding of poker in general.

Texas Hold'em is one of the many variations of poker. In all poker games, money is wagered on the outcome of each hand, but each variation of poker has its own structure for dealing cards, betting, and awarding the money wagered. *Winning money is the object of all poker games.* Without monetary stakes, poker is a meaningless game. Poker combines elements of both skill and luck. The structure of the game determines the extent to which skill is more of a factor than luck.

In cardrooms throughout the country, two variations of poker predominate—Seven-Card Stud and Texas Hold'em. Both variations require a high degree of skill to be successful. Only players with the knowledge, discipline, and patience to execute correct strategies will win over the long run.

Compared to Seven-Card Stud, Hold'em is characterized by

• More players: Unlike Seven-Card Stud, where a deck supports only seven players, in Texas Hold'em the deck can support 23 players. In practice, cardrooms seat up to 10 players at a Hold'em table.

• Faster play: More hands per hour are played in Hold'em because fewer cards are dealt from the deck. No more than 25 cards are dealt in a 10-player game. With a fast dealer, it is possible to play as many as 40 hands per hour.

• Less memorization: All exposed cards in Hold'em remain on the table. There is no need to remember the contents of previously folded hands.

•More competitive hands: The characteristic feature of Hold'em is the use of shared cards to make up a hand. Since most of your cards are also everybody else's, there will not be a great disparity between the strengths of the winning and losing hands.

Hold'em is a complex, exciting, and aggressive game. For both the recreational and serious gambler, mastering Hold'em is a source of much enjoyment and many rewards.

Part I

The Game of Texas Hold'em

This book begins with a discussion of how to play Texas Hold'em, covering the rules of the game (Chapter 1), the actual conduct of games in public cardrooms (Chapter 2), and online poker rooms (Chapter 3).

If you are completely new to Texas Hold'em, it is a poker variation that will seem strange at first. People with little knowledge of poker usually have a familiarity with *stud* and *draw* variations because of their portrayal in popular culture. Stud games "Five-Card" and "Seven-Card" are the most popular versions) deal hands that are a mix of cards known only to the holder and cards seen by everyone. As cards are dealt and bets placed, only the player has complete knowledge of his or her hand, but others make guesses based on partial knowledge from the exposed cards. For draw games (Five-Card Draw is the most popular), there are no exposed cards. Only betting patterns and the number of cards drawn for improvement provide information to the other players.

Texas Hold'em is in a completely different class of poker variants known as *flop* games. Flop games have elements of both stud and draw games. Like draw games, the cards dealt to the players are not exposed and are known only to them. Like stud games, hands are improved through exposed cards. The twist is that *the exposed cards belong to everyone*. The use of shared (or community) cards to complete a poker hand is the defining characteristic of flop games. Some of the other flop variants (Omaha, Omaha Eight or Better, and Pineapple) are described in Appendix I. Of the flop games, Texas Hold'em is the most intricate and challenging to play. The annual *World Series of Poker* uses Texas Hold'em to determine the champion. This book specifically addresses Texas Hold'em. While some of the information presented is relevant to the other flop games (and poker in general), the correct strategy and tactics for a game such as Omaha are different from Texas Hold'em, even though on the surface the games look remarkably similar.

Opportunities to play Texas Hold'em are more widespread than most people realize. Aside from the obvious locations (Atlantic City and Las Vegas), there are public cardrooms throughout California and the Northwest, on Native American reservations throughout the United States, and on riverboats up and down the Mississippi River system in the country's heartland. Chapter 2 describes what to expect in a public cardroom and how to conduct yourself. To locate a public cardroom near you—or near a place you plan to visit—check the listings in Chapter 10 for public cardrooms in the United States and Canada. The listings are sorted geographically and contain locations and contact information for 220 cardrooms.

The Internet has actually provided unlimited opportunity to play Texas Hold'em because of the growth of online poker games. Chapter 10 also profiles 15 online cardrooms where you can compete for real money. Chapter 3 discusses play in online cardrooms and the differences between playing poker "in person" and over the Internet against remote opponents.

Be aware that the legal issues surrounding online gambling are murky. **Discussion of online poker is for informational purposes only. In no way should anything in this book be construed as legal advice or an endorsement or guarantee of online services.** It is the reader's responsibility to know the appropriate laws governing any activity undertaken and to consult with a lawyer when unsure. Online poker play is covered in this book because the Internet—and the opportunities and risks brought by the Internet—are here to stay. It will become increasing difficult for the government to regulate online activities. Therefore, it is more important than ever to be informed and responsible when online.

1. Rules

The object of Hold'em is to accumulate money. As in any variation of poker, money is obtained by winning the *pot*—all the bets made during the course of a hand. There are two ways to win the pot:

• *Be the last remaining player.* During the play of a hand, players will fold and forfeit their interest in the pot. You win if you are the last remaining player.

• *Have the highest ranking hand.* If more than one player remains after the last round of betting, there is a *showdown.* All remaining players show the contents of their hands. If you have the highest-ranking hand, you win the pot.

A Hand in Hold'em

At the beginning of a hand, each player is dealt two cards face down—their *pocket cards.* During play of the hand, a total of five additional cards are exposed in the center of the table in three stages, creating the *board.* Each stage of dealing has a different name, and before each stage is a round of betting. There is a fourth and final round of betting after the last card.

> The *flop*—the first three exposed cards.
> The *turn*—the fourth card.
> The *river*—the fifth and last card.

In Hold'em, cards on the board are *community cards*—they are used by all the players in forming their hands. Your hand is the best five-card combination possible, using your two pocket cards and any of the five community cards. If the best five-card hand consists of the five cards on the board, that is your hand. Your pocket cards only matter if one or both of them improve what is on the board.

Hand Rankings

The recognized five-card combinations are summarized next in order of rank (the highest-ranked hand, which is the least likely to occur, is listed first). To reinforce the concept of pocket cards and community cards, a sample hand is shown for each hand ranking. Pocket cards are on the left, and the complementing community cards follow each description. Learn to spot patterns in the formation of hands. The use of community cards creates possibilities for hands in Hold'em that players of Seven-Card Stud don't think about. For example, in contrast to Stud, it is possible for two Hold'em players each to have three cards of the same rank. However, it is impossible for two Hold'em players to have flushes in different suits. These new possibilities and new limitations are discussed.

  STRAIGHT FLUSH—five sequentially ordered cards of the same suit. The value of the highest card determines the value of the straight flush. Therefore the highest-ranked hand possible is a *royal flush*: – A, K, Q, J, 10 (all of the same suit).

FOUR OF A KIND—four cards of the same rank, such as four 9s or four Aces. In Hold'em, at least one pair must appear on the board for someone to have four of a kind. For example: if you are dealt two 9s, the other two 9s must appear on the board for you to have four 9s. You can also have four 9s if three 9s appear on the board and you hold the remaining 9. If two pairs are on the board, it is possible for two players to have four of a kind. In this case, the rank of the cards forming the hand determines the rank of the hand (four 9s beat four 8s). If all four 9s appear on the board, then all players have four 9s as their hand. To win the hand in this circumstance, one of your pocket cards must be higher than anyone else's pocket card and higher than the fifth card on the board. This illustrates an important concept in Hold'em—the *kicker*. A kicker is a pocket card that is not part of the combination, but decides ties. If the fifth card on the board is higher than anyone's kicker, all players have the exactly the same hand and the pot is split.

  FULL HOUSE—A full house (also referred to as a *boat*) is three of one kind and two of another. For someone to have a full house, at least a pair must appear on the board. There are several card combinations that allow you to have a full house. One is to have a pair of pocket cards that match one card on the board and an unrelated pair also appears. A full house also occurs with two unmatched pocket cards when one matches a pair on the board and the other matches one of the other board cards. For example, you have two 4s as pocket cards and the board has 10, 10, 4, J, A (you have 4s full with 10s). Notice that in this case, you could lose to someone holding 10, A. They would have 10s full with Aces. That person could lose to someone with a pair of Jacks who would have Jacks full with 10s. When multiple players have full houses, the person with the highest three of a kind wins. The pair only comes into play when players have the same three of a kind. Given this board, a person holding A, 10 beats a player hold 10, J. Each player has 10s full, so the pairs play and the Aces beat the Jacks. A less common way to have a full house is when three of kind appears on the board and you hold a pair in the pocket. Again, if two or more people hold a pair in the pocket, the highest pair wins.

  FLUSH—five cards of the same suit. In Hold'em, at least three suited cards must appear on the board for someone to have a flush. Note that since only five cards appear on the board, it is not possible for two players in the same hand to have flushes in different suits. All flushes will be of the same suit and the highest card wins. For example: if three Hearts appear on the board, a person holding A, 2 of Hearts beats someone holding K, Q of Hearts. If four Hearts appear on the board, a person holding an A of Hearts, and a 2 of a different suit beats someone holding any other pair of Hearts, because only one card is needed to complete the flush. Having an Ace-high flush is referred to as having the *nut-flush*. Of course, if the board showed 3, 4, 5, 6 of Hearts, someone holding a 2 of Hearts beats someone holding an Ace since the 2 completes a straight flush.

STRAIGHT—five cards of differing suits in sequential order. The higher the rank of the top card, the higher the straight. The highest possible straight is an Ace-high straight (A, K, Q, J, 10) . The lowest possible straight is A, 2, 3, 4, 5 and is often referred to as a *bicycle* or *wheel*. At least three of the cards in the straight must come from the board.

 THREE OF A KIND—three cards of the same rank, also referred to as *trips* or a *set.* You have trips if a pocket pair matches one of the cards on the board, or if one of your pocket cards matches a pair on the board, or if three of a kind appears on the board. Note that more than one player can hold three of the same kind. If a pair of Aces is on the board, and you hold one Ace and an opponent holds the other Ace, you both have three Aces. If three of a kind appears on the board, all players have at least three of a kind.

  TWO PAIR—two cards of one rank in combination with two cards of a different rank. This is a very common hand in Hold'em and illustrates a concept discussed earlier—the kicker. Suppose the board shows K, K, 3, 7, 5. You hold J, 3 and another player holds a 10, 3. Both of you have two pair, Ks and 3s, but you win, since your J-kicker beats the 10-kicker. As mentioned before, it is possible for the top kicker to appear on the board, in which case the pot is split. Suppose for the same pocket cards, the board showed, K, K, 3, 7, A. Both of you have Ks and 3s with an Ace kicker. Your J does not get to play and the pot is split. When comparing hands with two pair, the top pair determines who wins. Which brings us to another important concept in Hold'em—the *overcard*. Suppose you have K,Q in the pocket and the board comes up K, 3, 3, Q, A. The Ace on the board is an overcard to your King. Your hand is two pair, Kings and Queens but you lose to anyone holding a single Ace in the pocket, since they also have two pair (Aces and threes).

ONE PAIR—two cards of the same rank. If you have two pocket cards of the same rank, you have one pair. If two cards of the same rank appear on the board, everyone has at least one pair. Any card you hold that matches at least one card on the board gives you one pair.

HIGH CARD—If none of the combinations described can be formed, the high card wins at showdown. If players share the same high card, the second highest card plays, and so on.

SPLIT POTS—Suits are not ranked in poker. If two or more players have the same five-card hand at showdown, the money is split between them.

Betting

A hand of Texas Hold'em has four rounds of betting. In a *limit* game (the most common form of Hold'em), the first two betting rounds are set at an arbitrary limit (such as $2), and the last two betting rounds are at twice the limit of the early rounds. All bets and raises must be in increments of the limit. Hold'em games are referred to by their limits. In a $2–4 limit game, the betting increments in the first two rounds are $2 and in the last two rounds $4. The flowchart on Page 10 shows the four betting rounds and the possible decisions in each round.

Seeding the Pot: Before any cards are dealt, two designated players must place *blind bets* to seed the pot. The player selected as the *small blind* must bet half the smaller limit. Then the player to the immediate left of the small blind, designated as the *big blind*, must bet the full amount of the smaller limit. In a typical $2–4 game, the small blind bet is $1 and the big blind bet is $2. After each hand, the blind positions shift by one seat.

Round 1—After the Deal: The first round of betting occurs after all players are dealt their pocket cards. Betting begins with the player to the immediate left of the big blind, who must *call*, meaning match the big blind bet in order to stay in the game. Betting proceeds to the left. To stay in the game, each player must call the current bet. All players, including the blinds, have the option of raising when it is their turn. *Raises*, which are a match and increase of the previous bet, are in increments of the big blind bet (if $2 is the blind bet, then all raises are in increments of $2). Usually, raises are capped at three: If three raises have been made, no further raising is allowed. When play reaches the small blind, that player must make up the difference between the small and big blind bets, plus any raises, to stay in the game. The big blind player has the option to raise (if the cap has not been reached) after all the other players have acted.

Round 2—After the Flop: After betting on the pocket cards is complete, the dealer exposes the first three community cards (the flop) on the table. In a $2–4 game, bets and raises after the flop are again in $2 increments. Betting starts with the small blind and continues to the left. The small blind may either bet or *check* (pass on making a bet). Because each player has the option of checking, it is possible for everyone to check after the flop, which will result in no additional money going into the pot. If a player checks and someone bets later on, the player who checked gets a turn to call the bet or even raise. Raising after checking is a play referred to as a *check-raise*. Once a bet is made, all players must at least call the bet to stay in the game, and raising is an option. To stay in the game, a player must call all bets and raises, which results in all remaining players contributing equally to the pot.

Round 3—After the Turn: After betting on the flop, a fourth card (the turn) is exposed on the board. Play again starts with the small blind who either checks or bets. As play proceeds to the left, the increments for bets and raises are doubled. In a $2–4 game, bets are $4 after the turn card and raises are in increments of $4.

Round 4—At the River: After the third round of betting, the fifth card (the river card) is exposed. There is a final round of betting at the same level as the turn card.

If more than one player remains after the fourth round of betting, there is a showdown. The player with the highest-ranked hand wins the pot.

Betting Structure of $2– 4 Texas Hold'em
Blinds: small – $1, big – $2.

Deal: receive two pocket cards.

Call $2 or Raise to $4 — No → Fold

Yes

Flop: three community cards exposed.
Act before a bet.   Act after a bet.

Check or Bet $2

Call $2 or Raise to $4 — No → Fold

Yes

Turn: fourth community card exposed.
Act before a bet.   Act after a bet.

Check or Bet $4

Call $4 or Raise to $8 — No → Fold

Yes

River: fifth community card exposed.
Act before a bet.   Act after a bet.

Check or Bet $4

Call $4 or Raise to $8 — No → Fold

Yes

Showdown: high hand wins.

Unique Features of Texas Hold'em

Hold'em has a small number of starting hands. Only 169 unique starting hands exist since many of the initial two-card combinations are equivalent. All suits are considered equal, so hands such as A♣ J♠ and A♥ J♦ are the same, and likewise, suited combinations such as A♦ J♦, A♠ J♠ are also equivalent hands.

Hold'em is a fixed position game. *Position* refers to the order in which players act in a round of betting. During a Hold'em hand, your position does not change. The small blind always acts first, the big blind second, the player to the left of the big blind next, and so on. In stud games, position changes as the cards are dealt since the player with the highest exposed cards acts first. Position is important because in all forms of poker, it is advantageous to act last in a round of betting. Your position at the start of a hand of Hold'em stays the same for all four rounds of betting, conferring either a permanent advantage or disadvantage.

In Hold'em, it is possible to have the nuts. The *nuts* is the highest possible hand that can be formed with a given set of community cards. For example, if you hold K♠ K♣, and the board has K♥ 10♦ 7♠ 5♣ 2♥, you can bet and raise to the maximum, knowing that you cannot be beat. No straights or flushes can be formed from this board, and, without a pair, neither can a full house or four of a kind. Your three Kings are the nuts. Suppose instead, with the same hand, K♠ K♣, the board has A♣ A♠ K♥ 7♥ 3♣. Even though you have a much higher hand than in the previous situation (Kings full with Aces), you can be beat. Someone holding A♥ K♦ wins with Aces full, but that is not the nuts. In this case, the nuts is A♦ A♥.

The winner takes all. In Hold'em, the highest ranking hand wins the pot. It is not a split-pot game like some variations of poker. Split pots in Hold'em occur only if two or more players have identical high hands at the showdown.

2. Texas Hold'em in a Cardroom

In a casino or public cardroom, poker games are dealt on a large, oval, felt-covered table. The table, shown in the figure below, seats the dealer and up to 10 players. There usually are no markings on the table.

The dealer sits in front of a tray of *chips*. A plastic circle, imbedded in the table to the right of the dealer, provides a spot for separating the cardroom's percentage of the pot, called the *rake*. There is a slot in the table where the dealer deposits cash from players that are buying in, and a box to the dealer's left where tips are placed.

A small plastic button is used to indicate which person acts last in

Table Layout

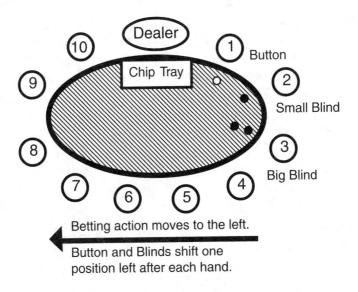

Betting action moves to the left.

Button and Blinds shift one position left after each hand.

the hand. The button starts with the player to the immediate left of the dealer. The person to the left of the button is the *small blind*, and the next person to the left is the *big blind*. Play proceeds from right to left: You act after the person on your right and before the person on your left. At the end of each hand, the button is passed to the next player on the left and the blind positions are shifted accordingly.

The dealer conducts the game. All players receive their cards from the dealer, and the dealer exposes the community cards. The dealer collects the bets from each player and, if necessary, makes change. Players never reach into the pot or handle any chips but their own. Players never handle any cards other than the two that are dealt to them. If there is a showdown at the end of the hand, the dealer inspects the hands and awards the pot to the player with the highest hand. In cardroom poker, *cards speak,* meaning that you do not have to state the contents of your hand. If you mistakenly state your hand, you still get the pot if your hand is the best. Always show your cards at the showdown and let the dealer inspect them. Pay attention in case the dealer makes a mistake.

Cardrooms make money from poker, either by taking a percentage from every pot (the rake) or by charging players for the time they spend at the table. In low-limit games ($5–10 and below) cardrooms take a rake, usually about 5% of the pot, up to a certain limit, such as $5. In higher limit games ($10–20 and above), cardrooms often charge players for table time instead of taking a rake. In a game paid for by a rake, the dealer takes the money after each round of betting and puts it in on the plastic circle on the table. After each hand the money is moved to the dealer's chip tray.

The rake is not an insignificant cost to players because poker is a zero-sum game—your loss is someone else's gain. Suppose there is a game with ten players starting with $100 each, resulting in $1000 on the table initially. If the players are evenly matched and never leave the table, money simply passes back and forth between them, with the cardroom taking a little each time. It's easy to see that if this game goes on indefinitely, the cardroom will end up with all the money. To make money at poker, not only do you have to be better than the other players, but you have to beat the rake. You must win enough money to afford to give about 5% to the cardroom and play in games with new money entering.

In addition to the cost of the rake, it is customary to tip the dealer. Tips are usually given by a player after winning a pot. Usually players give the dealer a $1 chip after a win. Tipping is not obligatory and for small pots $1 is a large cut and not always given. It is polite to tip dealers, but tips are another poker expense that need to be controlled for profit to be realized.

Joining a Game

Not all casinos have poker rooms, and not all casinos offering poker have Texas Hold'em. Call ahead to find out what games and betting limits are offered at the casinos that you plan to visit.

Betting Limits: Once you decide where to play, select a game with affordable limits. For a $3–6 game, you should have at least $100 in front of you. In a $5–10 game, you need at least $200. For higher-limit games, you need proportionally more money. It must be money you can afford to lose. Not even the best poker players make a profit every time they play. You cannot fear losing money or you won't be able to play correctly. Placing bets that lose is an integral part of the game. You cannot win in the long run without the ability to absorb losses along the way. If you are new to Hold'em, start with lower-limit games, even if you can afford higher ones. Players in higher-limit games are better. To make money at poker, you must not only have a sufficient bankroll to stay in the game, you must be better than your opponents. Learning poker by playing in high-limit games against expert players is a sure way to lose a lot of money fast.

Signing up to play: When you arrive at the cardroom, tell the manager what games you are interested in playing. They will put you on lists for those games. You can sign up for more than one game and play in the first one. You can also switch games later on. If you want to play $5–10 Hold'em, but that game has a waiting list, you can take an available seat in a $3–6 game. Ask the manager to notify you when a space in the $5–10 game becomes available.

Buying in: Most tables have a minimum buy-in. Before you begin to play, you must buy a minimum amount of chips, usually $50 in a low-limit game ($5–10 or less). Chips come in standard denominations that are color coded: $1 (white), $5 (red), $25 (green) and $100 (black). Occasionally, players will purchase chips from each other, but some cardrooms have rules against this. If there is a question, ask the dealer.

Table stakes: Most games are played *table stakes,* meaning you cannot reach into your pocket for additional money, or take money off the table during a hand. All your playing money must be on the table at the start of the hand. The money in front of you need not all be in chips. You can buy some chips and place additional money on the table in the form of bills. You may use those bills to purchase chips during a hand, but you cannot reach into your pocket for additional money.

All in: If you run out of money during the course of a hand, you are *tapped out,* and are allowed to go *all in.* When you go all in, you do not have to call any more bets to stay in the hand. If only one opponent remains, he or she cannot bet more money. The remaining cards are dealt and the person with the highest hand wins the pot. If you go all in against two or more opponents, they may continue betting. The money they bet goes into a separate pot, the *side pot,* for which you cannot compete. If one of your opponents has the highest-ranked hand at showdown, that person wins both pots. If you have the highest hand, you win only the main pot. The side pot goes to the person with the second highest hand. You may purchase chips after going all in, but it must be for at least the table minimum. You are allowed buy in (put more cash on the table or purchase more chips) any time between hands, but not during a hand.

Games in progress: When you join a game in progress, you will be required to *post* if you take a seat that the blind position has just passed. To post, you must place a bet equal to the big and small blinds combined in order to receive cards. This money goes into the pot in addition to the money from the current blinds. Like the big blind, you automatically get to see the flop, unless there are raises that you decide not to call. When joining a game in progress, you also have the option to wait until the blind position gets to you and then enter the game as a normal blind. Many people do this because it is cheaper in the long run and lets them observe the game before they play. The blind bets are your cost for receiving those initial pocket cards during the times you are not in the blind position.

Leaving the table during play: You are allowed to temporarily leave your seat. Either leave your chips on the table, or tell the dealer you are taking a break, and the dealer will hold your seat for a specified interval of time, usually a half-hour. No cards will be dealt to your spot unless you are seated at the table. If you miss your turn as a blind, the dealer marks your spot with a button that says "missed blind." When you return, you will be required to pay the missed blind to get back into the game, or you can wait for the blind to come back to you.

Leaving the game: You can leave a poker game at any time. Tell the dealer your seat is open, pick up your chips and take them to the cashier's window to exchange them. Dealers do not buy chips back from you.

General Conduct

Poker is a fast moving game, and for beginners, it is intimidating to play. Poker has many unspoken norms for behavior, and you risk quick ostracism if you violate them carelessly. If you are new, don't hesitate to ask questions of the dealer. Also, most poker players are friendly and will assist newcomers with proper conduct.

Don't pick up your cards: Leave your cards face-down on the table. Look at them by cupping your hands over them and turning up the corners. Get in the habit of looking at your cards once and leaving them face down. There are many other things to observe at the table, so avoid looking at your cards repeatedly. In addition, many cardrooms have rules against taking your cards off the table. Even where it is permissible, picking up and holding cards is still a bad habit to acquire. It is easy for the players next to you to see your cards if you are holding them in front of you.

Protect your cards: If you win a pot, return the cards to the dealer after the money is pushed to you. If you sit next to the dealer, leave a chip on top of your cards to prevent the cards from being accidentally scooped up. Once your cards are gone, you do not get them back.

Act in turn: Don't broadcast actions before it is your turn—such as reaching for chips or giving cards back to the dealer. If you fold before someone has a chance to bet, they don't have to worry about a raise from you. If you bet a good hand before people ahead of you have acted, they may fold, which costs you money. Acting out of turn gives information to opponents that they should not have.

Actions are to fold, check, bet, call, and raise: While most communication is non-verbal, all communication of your intended action, including verbal statements, is binding.
- To fold—Return your cards to the dealer. Do not expose them to anyone.
- To check—Tap the table with your hand.
- To bet or call—Place the money in front of you. State the amount if ambiguous.
- To raise—Place the money in front of you. State the amount if ambiguous, or if the dealer needs to make change from the pot.

Don't *splash the pot:* Always put bets in front of you where the dealer can clearly see the amount. Let the dealer handle the money and make change if necessary. If you throw your money directly into the pot, no one is absolutely sure if you bet the correct amount. The game will be interrupted while the dealer counts all the money in the pot, and the other players will be upset with you for causing the break in the action.

Don't make *string bets:* A string bet is where you call a bet and then reach back to your pile of chips to raise. You must place all the chips for raise at once, or state your intention to raise out loud.

Don't give information (especially after you've folded): This especially angers other players because it can have a big effect on a hand. If you threw away the A♦ and now there is a Diamond flush possible on the board, a person holding a King-high flush has the highest possible hand. If you comment out loud about throwing away the Ace, the person with the King can raise to the maximum, now knowing they can't be beat. If cards are exposed in any way (which happens occasionally by accident), everyone at the table must be shown the card. If you expose your cards to another player, all players at the table can demand to see your cards.

Don't delay the game: Pay attention. Act in a timely fashion when it is your turn.

Respect the dealer: If the dealer makes a mistake, be polite. If you have just received pocket Aces for example, and there is a misdeal before you have a chance to play them, do not give the dealer a hard time. The cards are not yours until everyone has been properly dealt. If the dealer makes a mistake that negates the deal, that is part of the game.

Rule Variations

Spread-limit **games:** Some cardrooms offer structured games where the betting is not in fixed increments. In a $5–10 spread-limit game, the allowed bets and raises are any amount up to $5 in the first two rounds, followed by any amount up to $10 in the second two.

No raising caps when head-to-head: Some cardrooms cap raises at three until there are two remaining players. Two players going head-to-head are allowed to have a raising war and raise as many times as they like.

Check-raise: A check-raise is allowed in almost all games, but a few places have rules against it. Remember, when in doubt, ask.

Structure variations: Different cardrooms can have variations on the traditional blind and betting-round structure. Some variations I have experienced include $2–$5–$5–$10, which means that if there are no pre-flop raises everyone pays $2 to see the flop, but must bet $5 to see the turn card. Bets then double again after the river card. I also played in a game that did not have a rake; instead the player on the button (the last player to bet in each round) paid the house an amount equal to one big blind. In exchange, that person was included in the hand, and unless there was a pre-flop raise, saw the flop without betting additional money. The first time you play in a cardroom, ask the poker manager to explain all the house rules and take notice of unfamiliar variations.

Jackpot games: Some cardrooms set aside a portion of the rake to form a jackpot that is awarded to players under special circumstances. The most common kind is the "bad-beat" jackpot—in order to win, a player must have a losing hand. The catch is that the losing hand must be ranked Aces-full or better. Since bad-beats of this nature are rare, jackpots can get enormous before someone wins and the jackpot rebuilds. I once witnessed a $4–8 Hold'em table on a Missouri riverboat hit a $20,000 jackpot. In that instance, the casino awarded the losing hand 50% ($10,000), the winning hand 25% ($5,000), and the remaining six players split the remaining 25%. Again, ask for the details before you play. If a casino has a jackpot, it will have house rules on which events hit the jackpot and how the pot is awarded.

Pot-limit **and** *No-limit* **Hold'em:** Some games do not have betting limits in each round. In any betting round, players may bet any amount up to the amount present in the pot (pot-limit), or in some games, any amount up to the chips they have in front of them on the table (no-limit). In real cardrooms, these kinds of games are usually at a high level for high stakes. Beginners and recreational players should avoid them. However, some online cardrooms offer pot-limit and no-limit games with small buy-ins that none of the players who joins the table can exceed. As a result, no one player has a large amount of money on the table at any one time. Under these conditions, recreational players can afford to learn and experience pot-limit and no-limit Hold'em. The "table stakes" rule—that no one can bet more than they have on the table—becomes the effective limit for these kinds of games.

3. Texas Hold'em Online

Any game that does not require physical contact can be played over the Internet. Board games such as chess and popular card games, including many poker variations, now have online playing venues and informational Web sites. This chapter describes how to get started playing poker online and discusses how the online experience differs from a public cardroom.

Online games have grown in popularity because the Internet has made it possible for real-time interactions to occur between groups of people scattered all over the world. The term "real-time" means that no significant delay occurs in the transmission of information to any location in the world. To understand the impact of the Internet on competitive activities, consider the example of chess players, who have for centuries recognized two distinct forms of competition. Players who meet in-person, sit at the same table, and take turns moving one set of chess pieces on one board, are said to engage in "over-the-board" competition. This is the most familiar version of chess, with the two players totally immersed until the game ends, usually in one sitting.

A less familiar form of competitive chess, although it appears to have existed throughout the history of chess, is "correspondence" chess. Two players compete without ever meeting in person or entering the same room. Each player uses his or her own chess set. Moves are communicated via the mail with long transmission delays. Because each player must act in turn, a single game usually takes one year or longer to complete. Obviously the players are not totally immersed in the game during the year and many activities that are forbidden in over-the-board competition—studying chess books, analyzing by actually moving the pieces about—are a normal part of correspondence play.

The real-time transmission of information on the Internet has blurred the distinction between correspondence chess and over-the-board chess. Two players in two widely separated locations can meet online at a "virtual" chess club and conduct a game in one sitting, at the same pace as a normal over-the-board game. However, it is important to note *that an online chess game is still a correspondence game.* The two players do not meet in person, they do not share the same chess set, and most importantly, they can talk to other people and refer to chess books. While this distinction between correspondence chess and over-the-board chess may appear off subject in a poker book, these models for chess are relevant to Internet poker. If you are considering online poker, remember that poker games played over the Internet are correspondence games. You will compete against unseen people in remote locations, who are able to engage in unseen activities (talk to others, refer to books, etc.).

Online Poker Rooms

As of this writing, online poker rooms operate from offshore locations. It is illegal to operate an online casino from within the United States, although the law on this is changing rapidly. Some casinos in Nevada are pressing for laws allowing their United States-based businesses to operate over the Internet. The law on playing in online casinos for real money is unclear. **In no manner should this book be construed to offer legal advice on the issue of online gambling.** The law in this area is vague and changing. It is your responsibility to know and follow the laws that apply in your state and jurisdiction. Seek appropriate legal advice from a qualified attorney if unsure.

It is my opinion that observation of real-money play in online poker rooms and participation in play-money games are valuable activities for learning the structure, mechanics, and strategies of various forms of poker. However, playing for real money in an online venue is a risky activity. It is difficult to know for certain if the games and operators are completely legitimate. If you choose to play poker online, proceed with caution.

Setting Up To Play Online

To play poker online, you will need:

• A computer
• A software package called a *Web browser*
• A connection to the Internet.

I will make some general comments on all of the above; in particular, how your choices relate to online poker games. It is not my intent to review specific computers or make recommendations. Consumer choice changes weekly and there are thousands of publications on computers, software, and accessories for those who need guidance.

Computers: Personal computers come in two basic types that are defined by their operating system. The operating system is the program that appears when you first turn on the computer and allows the user to perform all the basic tasks—launch application programs, manage files, connect to peripherals. The Windows® operating system published by Microsoft runs on more than 90% of the personal computers manufactured. The Macintosh® operating system runs only on computers manufactured by Apple® Computer and accounts for less than 10% of the market. There are other operating systems (for example Unix and its variants), but most people rarely encounter them. Windows dominates the market so most online poker rooms require use of a Windows-based computer. If your primary purpose for owning a computer is for online activity, poker or otherwise, a Windows-based computer will give you more online options.

The Macintosh operating system is used heavily for education, graphics design, and desktop publishing (this book was produced on a Macintosh). If you have an Apple computer, you can still play online poker, but your choices will be limited. While all online poker rooms work on Windows machines, not all work on a Macintosh. The online cardroom profiles in Chapter 10 specify which ones are Macintosh compatible.

Web browser: The software that allows you to download and view Web pages is called a *Web browser*. The most popular browsers are Netscape® and Microsoft's Internet Explorer®. While these two browsers are slightly different in appearance, they are nearly identical in function. Use of one or the other is a matter of personal preference. Most computers come with at least one of these browsers (often both) preloaded. Once you are using a browser to surf the Web, the difference between the Windows and Macintosh operating systems is not readily apparent. From the user's point of view, Internet Explorer works close to the same way in either operating system. The same is true of Netscape. Once your Web browser is launched, you go to specific Web sites by typing the Uniform Resource Locator (URL) into the window at the top of the screen. The URL is the Web address that usually begins with http://www. For example http://www.sambraids.com will take you to my Web site assuming you have established an Internet connection.

Internet connection: By itself, your computer will not connect to the Internet. You must subscribe to an Internet Service Provider (ISP) to have access to the Web and other Internet features such as e-mail. There are two basic kinds of Internet service: dial-up and broadband. Dial-up subscriptions range between $15 to $25 per month and work over your existing phone line. You connect the cable that goes into your phone, into your computer instead and program the computer to dial the phone number provided by your ISP. Dial-up connections are inexpensive and easy to set up. The disadvantages are that they tie up your existing phone line and are slow, unstable, and unreliable. For real-time poker, the transmission delays and sudden disconnects in the middle of hands are a nuisance. Online poker games are programmed as a courtesy to automatically put players "all in" if, when it is their turn, they don't respond within 30 seconds. What going "all in" means is that a player does not have to match further bets to contest the pot. If the disconnected player's hand is the winning hand, his or her account is awarded the fraction of the pot present at the time of the disconnection. Bets placed after the disconnection go into a side pot and are awarded to the second-best hand. However, the "all in" courtesy is usually extended only once per day to avoid intentional disconnects motivated by players who want to finish the hand without paying.

Broadband connections are faster and more stable. However, they are more expensive ($40 to $60 per month), more difficult to set up, not available in all areas of the country, and not completely free of glitches. Your broadband connection will also experience sudden disconnects, though not as often as a dial-up. Broadband ISP's include providers that connect through the cable TV lines with use of a cable modem, and providers that work through the local phone company by using ISDN (Integrated Services Digital Network) or DSL (Digital Subscriber Line) services. Find out what services are available in your area and their set-up costs and procedures. Set up of a broadband connection is more complicated than plugging the phone line into your computer and entering a number. Often the set up takes several weeks and requires an on-site visit from a technician. Unless you live in a densely populated area, dial-up may be your only choice. If broadband is available and you try it, you will quickly get addicted to the increased download speeds. You will also not tie up your phone line. If you are a serious Internet user, consider getting broadband. The extra cost (compared to dial-up) is about the cost of the extra phone line that you might want if you spend hours online using a dial-up connection. If you are just getting started, try dial-up first and find out what the Internet is about.

One final note on Internet service for users of WebTV deserves mention. Televisions do not have computer processors and hard drives and therefore cannot download and run poker playing software. WebTV users are only able to view (browse) sites. You cannot play in any online poker room that requires a software download unless you have a computer.

Conduct of Online Games

The usual method in which online games operate is for the participant to download software from the poker room's Web site, that runs locally on the user's computer. Each online poker room has its own proprietary software. Most poker rooms require the user to download software that runs in a Windows environment, meaning that the choices of online poker rooms for the Macintosh user are limited. One notable exception is Pokerroom.com. Their URL is http://www.pokerroom.com. Pokerroom software runs entirely from within a Web-browser, using scripts written in the Java® programming language. The Java-based method is completely cross-platform. A participant in games at http://www.pokerroom.com can use any Windows-based or Macintosh computer with a Web-browser current enough to support Java scripts. It is not necessary to install additional software, an advantage for people who do not always use the same computer when going online.

Once you register and download the required software, you usually can observe games in progress and participate in play-money games against other online players. When the software is in operation, it provides you with a real-time view of the games in progress through animations complete with sound effects. First you are presented with a window listing all active games, betting limits, number of active players and available seats, and play or real money status. When you choose a game, a graphic of a poker table is displayed with the button, cards, and chips. Your cards and the community cards are displayed face up to you; the other players' cards are face-down. A menu of action buttons appears on your screen. When it is your turn, you point and click with your mouse to one of the actions— *Check, Fold, Call, Bet, Raise.*

Each online poker room has its own software with its own look and feel. You can try out several poker rooms to see which interface is more comfortable. I recommend a lot of practice in play money games before opening a real money account. Online poker has a different "feel" to it than in-person poker. For example, it is not possible to verbally state your intentions online. If you accidentally move the mouse-pointer a little too far over and click the fold button when you meant to hit raise, your hand is gone.

Surprisingly, online poker games often move faster than in a cardroom: 45–50 hands per hour are not uncommon. While slow, unstable Internet connections often put a drag on the game, there are many time-saving features of online games that make up for the delays. The software instantly handles routine tasks. It will shuffle cards, issue chips, give change, award pots, and determine the winning hand. All these actions take time for a real dealer to perform. As a result, online play requires greater attention on your part, since most of your waiting is for other players to act, which means you must be ready when they are. In a real cardroom, most of the down-time is waiting for the dealer, whose actions do not require your careful attention.

To play for real money, you create an account with the poker room of your choice and deposit money either directly with a credit card, or through an intermediary service such as NETeller® (http://www.neteller.com), Firepay® (http://www.firepay.com), or a prepaid ATM card (http://www.prepaidatm.com). The advantage of an intermediary is that your credit card information is never given to the casino, and some credit card companies block the use of their cards at online casinos. Online casinos usually encourage the use of an intermediary service, since they do not want to handle payment of the merchant's credit card processing fee or worry about charge-backs. Once your account is open, with money deposited, you can play in the real-money games.

If you are wary about using your credit card online, you can get a prepaid credit card. Go to http://www.mycard.com and follow the instructions on how and where to purchase a prepaid credit card. The user pays cash to a local store and receives a credit card good for the amount of cash paid and no more. Once charges equal to the amount of cash deposited are completed, the card is either discarded or reloaded by depositing more cash. No one can steal the number and ring up more charges than you have already prepaid. Nor can anyone ruin your credit rating since there is no line of credit.

There are two major problems unique to online real-money play that necessitate that each online poker room establish and enforce a policy. One is the unreliability of Internet connections. No one would play online if the possibility existed of losing a large pot with a monster hand because of a sudden disconnect. To protect players against such an occurrence, online poker rooms typically have a rule that automatically places players all-in should their connection to the game suddenly vanish. If you are suddenly locked out of a game because of a faulty Internet connection and have what turns out to be the winning hand, you still win all the money wagered up to the point you left. Of course, such a rule can also be abused. You could disconnect yourself whenever you wanted to try to draw someone out without having to call bets. To avoid abuse of all-in rules, the poker rooms usually limit their application to an individual to no more than once per day. If you are forced to go all-in because of an interruption, you lose the protection of the rule if you immediately resume play. Read the all-in policy carefully before you play in an online poker room.

The second major problem is the possibility of collusion between players. Because of the remote and anonymous nature of the Internet, it is possible for participants in a game to all be together in the same room, or in communication via telephone, so that they can share information and defraud the honest players in the game. Online poker rooms use software that records the events of every hand and searches for suspicious betting patterns. The software flags players who appear to be in collusion. Warnings are posted threatening to permanently ban players caught colluding, and all online rooms post vigorous assurances of the integrity of their games. It is not possible to know how much of a problem online collusion is or the effectiveness of the detection methods that are employed. Be wary of the game circumstances as you play. If something feels wrong, even if you cannot articulate what is wrong, get out and find another game. Chapter 10 has information as of February 2003 on some popular online poker rooms. Remember that the Internet is a dynamic place. Changes occur frequently. Go to http://www.intelligentpoker.com for updates.

Differences Between Online and In-person Poker

With the growth of online poker, much can be written comparing the experience of online poker to that of a real cardroom. If you have tried one venue and not the other, or must decide in which venue to begin, here are some general considerations.

Much lower limit games exist online than are found in a real cardroom. You can start your real-money poker career online much cheaper than in a real cardroom. It is possible to find $0.25–0.50 Hold'em games online, whereas stakes that low would never produce enough profit for the house in a real cardroom (the lowest limit games found in real cardrooms are usually $2–4).

Online play has much less overhead than a real cardroom. As a result, it is easier to be more selective about the games you choose to join. If you go to a real cardroom, you must incur the travel expenses. For many people, the travel is out-of-town with expenditures required for airline, taxis, dining, and overnight stay. Even if you live close to a real cardroom, it costs money to drive your car and park. At the tables, waitresses will provide drinks and snacks, for which they expect a tip. Dealers also expect a tip from each pot that you win. All of these expenses are in addition to the rake the casino takes for conducting the game. To profit from play in a real cardroom, all of these expenditures constitute overhead that must be paid from your winnings before a profit is realized.

Psychologically, overhead makes it difficult to be selective with the games in which you choose to compete. All poker books stress the need for choosing the right game, one that is within your betting limits and populated with enough poor players to be profitable. Much has been written on choosing the right seat at the right game. But suppose after spending substantial time and money getting to a cardroom, you can't find an ideal seat at a good game. Naturally, you will play in the available seat in whatever game is underway.

Another feature of online play is the impossibility of violating conduct rules during play. You cannot act out of turn, place string bets, see other player's cards, show your cards to others, or squirrel money away unseen in a table-stakes game. The software rigidly enforces the rules of the game and precisely displays all the game parameters. At all times, you know precisely the number of active players, how much money each has, and how much money is in the pot.

In the privacy of your home, you can have poker charts and tables open to aid in your decision-making, and make notes as you play. It is easy to know the exact pot odds (a concept that will be discussed in the next chapter) when you bet because the exact amount in the pot is displayed and you can tape a chart on odds from this book above your computer screen. The chart in Chapter 4—*Minimum Pot Size for Correct Pot Odds*—is especially useful for online play. When online, there is no one blowing smoke in your face, an uncomfortable distraction to many. If you do smoke, no one will complain or ask you to move.

In contrast, poker in a cardroom is a social event. Players talk, joke, and get angry with one another. If you get confused, people help you out. The waitress brings drinks and snacks. The dealers switch tables frequently and banter with the players. There is sensuality in a cardroom that fancy graphics and sound effects cannot create on a computer screen: the feel of the weight of real chips when you bet, the stiff shiny cards that you lift slightly off the table to view, the many kinds of people that play poker—all races, ages, professions, and economic backgrounds.

The social environment of a cardroom also means you can observe mannerisms and gestures that are clues to your opponents' thoughts, which are called *"tells."* Is someone who was staring off into space now paying close attention? Is someone so anxious to bet that their chips are in hand well before it is their turn? Is someone visibly disgusted with the river card? Obviously, none of this is observable online. However, that does not mean online play is completely free of "tells." Online players have their own response rhythms that will vary with the decisions they make. Most poker room software allows the player to click an action button at any time before their turn, even though the action will not be executed until it is their turn. Preplanned actions show up as instant responses, a possible "tell" that the player had an easy decision to make. Players may also use the instant response buttons as a bluff. Player personalities, as manifested by their betting patterns, are discernable in any environment. A player who bets aggressively is obvious both online and in-person. My recommendation is that if you are learning poker, go online and check out the resources. Participate in play-money games as a way of learning the mechanics and structure of the game. However, the first time you play for real money, do so in-person, in a cardroom surrounded by people you can observe and talk to. Do not play online until you have developed a good poker sense and can know immediately if the game situation is not working for you. However, once you are comfortable with poker and know yourself and your limits, online poker allows you to play anytime from anywhere.

Part II

Winning Poker

Mastering Texas Hold'em, like mastering any competitive activity, requires three kinds of knowledge: factual (Chapter 4), tactical (Chapter 5), and strategic (Chapter 6).

Factual knowledge includes the vocabulary, basic concepts, and sought-after goals that define the activity. Without the facts, you cannot make sense of the game. A golfer must know the difference between an iron, a wood, and a putter, and why all three are in a golf bag. Facts are learned by committing them to memory.

Tactics are the various actions taken to achieve the goals. Tactical knowledge is acquired through practice. You play the game and, through experience, gradually obtain the skills necessary for success. Golfers learn to swing their clubs and read the greens by repetitive practice.

Strategic knowledge is obtained after the facts are memorized and the tactical skills are acquired. Strategy is learning to see the game in a broad context. Once you possess strategic knowledge, your actions are no longer a direct response to individual events, but are considered in the context of a broad purposeful plan. Only after you reach the level of strategic thinking can you truly master a game. Great golfers don't play individual holes. They think about the course as a whole.

While I have used golf as an example, any activity that involves performance requires these three kinds of knowledge. Musicians have the factual knowledge of how to read music, the tactical knowledge of how to play their instrument, and the strategic knowledge of how to interpret the music. The facts, tactics, and strategies must be learned in order. It is not possible to shortcut the learning process by skipping ahead to strategy without learning facts and tactics, nor is it possible to learn music, golf, or poker from reading alone. You must play.

This section of the book presents the facts, tactics, and strategies of Texas Hold'em. The underlying theme is that you win at poker by making better decisions than your opponents make because over time, cards (and hence situations) are equally distributed. Poker decisions are based on five factors: your cards, your position, the number of opponents, the cost, and how your opponents play. The factual basis for each decision factor is presented first. How these facts enter into tactical play will then be discussed. Strategy is learning to give some factors more weight than others, depending on the game conditions. To plan strategy, you must learn to analyze the reasons and motivations for a poker game. In essence, poker is a social game. The competition for money takes place within a social context that must be understood before a correct strategy can be formulated.

4. Facts

The key to making intelligent poker decisions is to understand that successful poker is not about winning hands, it is about winning money. Since everyone has the same chance of being dealt a winning hand, winning hands are, in the long run, equally distributed among the players. Over time, money is accumulated by the players who make the best decisions.

Poker decisions require knowledge of mathematical probabilities, but the game is far more complex and cannot be completely described mathematically. In blackjack, where the dealer always plays the same way, it is possible to calculate the best decision for each hand. No such calculation is possible in poker because you are competing against different players, each of whom plays their own way. Not only do individual players differ, but each poker table develops its own group dynamics that changes as players enter and leave the game. The replacement of a single passive player with an aggressive one can instantly alter the mood of a poker table and necessitate changes in decision making.

The combination of mathematics, psychology, and social dynamics makes poker a rich and fascinating game. Mastering poker requires hours and hours of playing in different settings with different people. However, many people place too much emphasis on the psychological aspects of the game. They think poker is all about bluffing and reading body language. The fact is, poker has an underlying strategy that must be followed for there to be any chance of survival, let alone winning.

Correct strategy bases decisions on the knowledge available to you of the cards and your opponents. You never have perfect knowledge of your opponents, their cards, and the cards to come. Given imperfect information, you must assess what is most likely to happen. Decisions must be based on the most probable outcome of a hand, not on what you hope will happen.

Before discussing the actual play of hands, it is necessary to have the facts that intelligent decisions are based on. This section, which is meant to be used as a reference, contains tables, graphs, and summaries of important information and concepts. There are five factors to consider in every poker decision. After summarizing the five decision factors, each one is discussed in detail. How knowledge of these factors translates into actual play is the subject of the next chapter.

The Five Decision Factors

The decisions you make during the course of a hand should always take the following five factors into consideration:

Your cards—Betting in poker means you wager that, at showdown, your hand will be ranked the highest. Unless you believe that to be a likely possibility, you should not bet. Statistically, in a ten-handed game, you will only have the highest hand 10% of the time. Knowing when it is your time to have the best hand is of course the difficulty. When you have a strong hand, bet aggressively and force the other players to chase you. It is rarely correct to slow-play; that is, not bet a strong hand. If you don't have a strong hand, fold. In poker, money saved is the same as money won, and staying out of the 90% of the hands you are destined to lose is as important as being in the hands you win.

Your position is an extremely important factor in Hold'em since it is a fixed-position game. When you are in an early position (close to the blind) you have no way of knowing how large the pot will be at the end of a betting round, and how many players will be contesting it. To compensate for this disadvantage, you need to play stronger cards than you would from later positions.

The number of players contesting a pot determines the kinds of hands that are playable. The irony is that you can play weaker starting cards when many players contest the pot, but you must have a stronger final hand at showdown. A high pair is a strong favorite to win against one or two opponents, but if ten players enter the hand, someone is likely to beat a high pair with a flush or a straight. Conversely, drawing hands (weak initial cards that may give you a flush or straight) are playable against a large field since the final pot will be large, but drawing hands are seldom worth playing for small pots against one or two players.

Pot odds are the costs of staying in the hand compared to the pot size. In each betting round, you decide if the amount of money it will cost you to finish the round is worth the size of the pot being contested. The cost to play can range from nothing (if everyone checks) to three large bets (if there is a lot of raising late in the game). Like any sound investment decision, riskier plays must have greater rewards for success.

Opponents' playing styles—During the hands that you don't enter, observe the playing style of each player and of the group as a whole. Does a certain player only bet when he has good cards or does he bet with anything? Does a player buy-in for a small amount of money and carefully guard it, or does she buy new chips from the dealer frequently? For the table as a whole, are showdowns frequent or rare? A big mistake beginning poker players make is playing only their cards and not considering how other people are playing theirs. Your opponents' actions are a source of information that must be used.

Over the course of a hand, some of these factors become more important than others. Early in the hand, your position, the initial strength of your cards and the potential number of opposing players are the most important factors. Later in the hand, pot odds and the playing styles of the remaining players are more important. What follows is a detailed discussion of these five factors.

Your Cards

To succeed at Hold'em, you must have the ability to judge the winning potential of the first two cards you are dealt (your pocket cards). There are exactly 1326 equally probable combinations for two cards dealt from a deck of 52. However, because the suits are all equally ranked, the number of unique starting hands is reduced to 169. Not all 169 starting hands occur with the same frequency because the number of combinations required to produce each unique starting hand differs. For example, of the 1326 combinations, six result in AA, four result in AK suited, and 12 result in AK unsuited. In terms of percent, this means the chance for AA is 0.45%, AK suited is 0.30%, and AK unsuited is 0.90%.

To compute probabilities, it is useful to divide the 169 starting hands into five distinct groups. The groups and the number of hands in each group are *pairs* (13), *straight flush draws* (46), *straight draws* (46), *flush draws* (32), and *no draws* (32). Each group is based on what type of hand can be built when initial cards are combined with favorable community cards. The chart below summarizes the five groups and their frequency.

Frequencies of Starting Hands

Starting Hand	Frequency	Description
Pairs	5.9%	Two cards of the same rank.
Straight Flush Draws (SFD)	13.9%	Two suited cards that are also part of a straight. The hand 10♥ 8♥ is a straight flush draw (the flop could come up J♥ 9♥ Q♥).
Straight Draws (SD)	41.6%	Two cards that form part of a straight, but not a flush. With 10♥ 8♣ only a straight is possible after the flop.
Flush Draws (FD)	9.7%	Two suited cards that cannot form a straight..
No Draws (ND)	28.9%	Two cards that cannot be used as part of a straight or flush. For example Q♥ 4♣.

Subcategories of starting hands can be identified within these five groups. For example, a hand that contains two of the top five cards such as Ace, K, Q, J, or 10 is an Ace-high straight draw. The subcategories of starting hands can be grouped into roughly four categories of strength. The strength of a starting hand, identified in the table below, is described as premium, strong, drawing, or garbage.

Strength Categories of Starting Hands

Strength	Description	Examples
Premium	Hands that can win on their own.	Big pairs—AA, KK, QQ, JJ, 10 10; straight draws with aces such as A♣K♣, A♥ K♦.
Strong	Hands that will probably need improvement to win.	Medium pairs—99, 88, 77; Ace-high straight draws such as K♥Q♦; Royal Draws such as K♥J♥.
Drawing	Hands that will need help from the board to win.	Little pairs—66, 55, 44, 33, 22; connected straight flush draws such as 5♦6♦; Ace-high flush draws such as A♥7♥.
Garbage	Should not be played.	All other hands not listed above.

Patience is required to play Hold'em because you rarely receive premium and strong starting cards. The next table summarizes the frequency of selected premium and strong starting cards.

Frequencies of Selected Starting Hands

Starting Hand	Frequency (%)	Odds Against
AA	0.45	220-1
KK	0.45	220-1
AK (mixed or suited)	1.2	82-1
Any Premium Pair A A-10 10	2.3	43-1
Any Royal Draw	3.0	32-1
Any Ace-Face Combination	3.6	27-1
Any Ace High Flush Draw (Including Royals)	3.6	27-1
Any Ace High Straight Draw	14.3	6.0-1
Any Hand with an Ace (Including AA)	15.4	5.5-1

Your Position

You must play starting cards appropriate for your position. In an early position, you are forced throughout the hand to make decisions with the least amount of information. For example, if before the flop, you call the blind with a drawing hand, you could be faced with a raise from one or more players with premium pairs. Since you don't know what raises you will be faced with, don't play cards from an early position that are too weak to justify calling a raise.

Compared to Seven-Card Stud, the importance of position in Hold'em is one of the key differences between the games. Position changes throughout the hand in Stud. The critical factor in determining a playable stud hand isn't position, but rather, how "live" is the hand. If your first three cards in Seven-Card Stud are A, J, J and you look at the board and see the other two Jacks and one other Ace, you have a "dead" hand. The Jacks with Ace-kicker may look pretty, but your action should be to fold.

However, in Hold'em, only three cards initially appear on the board and they are your cards. To know when your hand is "dead" is more difficult in Hold'em because fewer cards are exposed. To judge if your Hold'em hand is "live," you must observe the bets from the other players. Therefore, position matters, and since your position stays fixed throughout the hand, you know ahead of time the betting order for the entire hand.

Associate the value of strength categories of starting hands with your position as measured from the big blind.

Position Recommendations for Starting Hands

Position	Seat Relative to Button	Playable Hands
Early-position	(seats 1-3)	premium hands
Mid-position	(seats 4-6)	premium and strong hands
Late-position	(seats 6-9)	premium, strong and drawing hands

What the position chart tells you is that the later your position, the more kinds of hands are potentially playable. Drawing hands increase in value with later positions, because more information (number of players, potential pot size) is available. The chart does not mean you should always play a drawing hand from a late position. It means that if other decision factors are favorable—factors that are only known from having a late position—a drawing hand is playable.

Number of Players

It is a general truth, that for all premium starting cards, the more players dealt in the hand, the more likely it is someone else will have at least as good a starting hand. The effect of the number of players dealt in the hand on the probabilities is most clearly seen by calculating the occurrences of high-ranked pocket pairs. If you hold a pocket pair, the chart below summarizes the odds against one or more players at the table holding a higher-ranked pocket pair.*

The chart shows that in short handed games, premium pocket pairs increase in value. If you hold JJ and are up against two opponents (a deal of 3), the odds against one or both of them having a higher pocket pair are 33-1. These are the same odds against KK competing with AA in a deal of seven hands.

Odds for Multiple Pocket Pairs

Your Hand	Number of Players Dealt in the Hand (Including You)								
	2	3	4	5	6	7	8	9	10
KK	200-1	100-1	67-1	50-1	40-1	33-1	29-1	25-1	22-1
QQ	100-1	50-1	33-1	25-1	20-1	16-1	14-1	12-1	11-1
JJ	67-1	33-1	22-1	16-1	13-1	11-1	9-1	7.8-1	6.9-1
10, 10	50-1	25-1	16-1	12-1	9.5-1	7.9-1	6.7-1	5.8-1	5.1-1
9, 9	40-1	20-1	13-1	9.5-1	7.5-1	6.2-1	5.2-1	4.5-1	3.9-1

* Computations performed using the methods of Brian Alspach, described in his paper on "Multiple Pocket Pairs" at http://www.math.sfu.ca/~alspach/comp35. and published in *Poker Digest*, Vol. 5, No. 2, January 2002.

The pattern shown in the previous chart, of premium cards being less likely to hold up as the number of players increases, is also true as the hand progresses. The more players that compete for pot, the more likely it is that the best hand will be out drawn. The best starting hand in Hold'em, AA, is always more likely to win than any other starting hand. However, the absolute probability of AA winning decreases as the number of players in the hand increases.

Pot Odds

Pot odds are the ratio of the amount of money in the pot to the amount it costs to stay in the hand. For example, when you bet $10 to contest a $100 pot, your bet is paid off 10:1 if you win. That ratio (the pot odds) should be greater than the odds against winning. For a flush draw with one card to come, the odds are 4:1 against making the flush. Calling when you are on a flush draw and the pot odds are 10:1 is a good bet. Calling in the same situation when the pot odds are 2:1 is a bad bet. Your odds of winning the hand haven't changed, but the payoff has, and that should determine the decision. *Poker is about winning money, not about winning hands.*

The tables and graphs that follow provide the statistical data you need to compute the pot odds both before and after the flop. The tables and graphs communicate three main points. The points are:

- Straights and flushes are rare after the flop. Unless there are a large number of players entering the hand, you rarely will have the correct pot odds to play only for a straight or flush.

- Unless you have a 10 or higher in your hand, you rarely will have the best hand after the flop. You are not getting good pot odds to enter a hand with low cards.

- The person with the best hand after the flop is a favorite to win. For almost all common drawing situations, odds of improvement on the draw are less than 50%.

Probabilities on the Flop

The tables on the next page show the probabilities of having a particular ranked hand after the flop. The first table presents probabilites for starting hands in the pairs, flush draw, and no draw groups. Straights and straight flushes are not possible after the flop for starting hands in these groups. Of course any two cards could improve to a straight or straight flush later on in the hand if the right cards appear.

For starting hands in the straight draw and straight flush draw groups, the probabilities on the flop are more complicated to summarize. Connected starting cards, such as 9-8, are more likely to flop a straight than gapped cards, such as 9-7. To summarize the probabilities, straight draws and straight flush draws must be separated into four groups: connected (such as 9-8), one-gap (such as 9-7), two-gap (such as 9-6), and three-gap (such as 9-5). A three-gap straight draw, such as 9-5, can only make one straight on the flop (9 high). Connected cards such as 9-8 have four straight possibilities on the flop (Q - high, J - high, 10 - high, 9 - high). Each straight possibility has a 0.3265% chance of occurring. Therefore 0.3265% times the number of straight possibilities gives the chance of a straight on the flop. The second table on the next page shows the probabilities after the flop for the different straight draw categories.

The third table shows the probabilities for starting cards that are straight flush draws. In this case, the probabilities for straights are slightly reduced when compared to straight draws, and the probabilities for flushes slightly reduced when compared to flush draws. The reason is that a small fraction of the possible straights and flushes will be straight flushes.

Note that even when they are possible, straights and flushes on the flop occur, at most, about 1% of the time, usually less. Also pay attention to the note at the bottom of the page, on Ace-high and Ace-low straight draws. The hand AK, for example, is a three-gap straight draw. Only one straight (Ace-high) is possible after the flop.

Probabilities on the Flop for Five-card Hands

NO STRAIGHT POSSIBLE

	After the Flop the Probability (in percent) of Having:							
Starting Hand	Straight Flush	Four of Kind	Full House	Flush	Straight	Three of Kind	Two Pair	One Pair
Pair	—	0.245	0.980	—	—	10.77	16.16	71.84
FD	—	0.010	0.092	0.842	—	1.571	4.041	40.41
ND	—	0.010	0.092	—	—	1.571	4.041	40.41

STRAIGHT DRAWS

	After the Flop the Probability (in percent) of Having:							
Starting Hand	Straight Flush	Four of Kind	Full House	Flush	Straight	Three of Kind	Two Pair	One Pair
Connected	—	0.010	0.092	—	1.306	1.571	4.041	40.41
One-gap	—	0.010	0.092	—	0.980	1.571	4.041	40.41
Two-gap	—	0.010	0.092	—	0.653	1.571	4.041	40.41
Three-gap	—	0.010	0.092	—	0.327	1.571	4.041	40.41

STRAIGHT FLUSH DRAWS

	After the Flop the Probability (in percent) of Having:							
Starting Hand	Straight Flush	Four of Kind	Full House	Flush	Straight	Three of Kind	Two Pair	One Pair
Connected	0.020	0.010	.092	0.837	1.286	1.571	4.041	40.41
One-gap	0.015	0.010	.092	0.832	0.964	1.571	4.041	40.41
Two-gap	0.010	0.010	.092	0.827	0.643	1.571	4.041	40.41
Three-gap	0.005	0.010	.092	0.821	0.321	1.571	4.041	40.41

Important: All straight draw starting hands with an Ace fall in the three-gap category because only one straight is possible. The hands AK, AQ, AJ, AT, A5, A4, A3, A2 all require three specific ranked cards to make the straight, the same as the hand 9-5. The hands KQ, KJ, 4-2, and 3-2, fall into the two-gap category because they cannot form straights higher than Ace-high or lower than Ace-low. For the same reason the hands QJ and 4-3 are in the one-gap category.

Importance of High Cards

The figure below shows the probability that at least one overcard—a card on the board higher than either card in your starting hand—will appear after the flop. The probabilities range from 100% (if the highest card in the starting hand is a 2) to 0% (for an Ace in the starting hand). The figure demonstrates that holding an 8 as a high card is not much different than holding a 2. Since straights and flushes are rare, pairing pocket cards with cards in the flop is much more likely than any other event. To win over the long run, you must play high cards because that decreases the chance that an opponent will pair with an overcard.

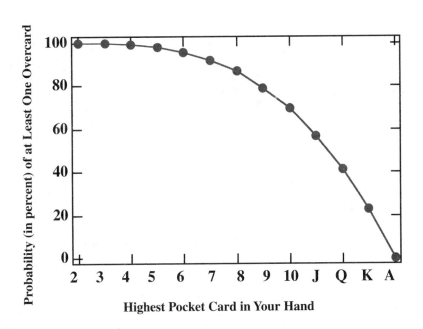

Probabilities for an Overcard on the Flop

Common Draws

After the flop, it is the number of unseen cards that can improve a hand (*outs*) which determine the probability of improvement on the turn or river. For example, if you have an open-ended straight draw, eight cards are out that will improve your hand to a straight (four of each rank on each end). With two cards to come, you have a 31.5% chance of making the straight, but with one card to come, the chance drops to 17.4%. Below is a tabulation of common draws and the chances of improvement. Knowing these probabilities is essential for computing the pot odds when betting on the turn and river cards. For situations not listed above, count the number of outs to make the hand and read the percentage next to the number of outs.

Probabilities for Improving a Hand

Probabilities in Percentages for Improving a Hand After the Flop

Situation	Improve to	Outs	Two cards to come	One card to come
Open ended SFD	Straight or Flush	15	54.1	32.6
Inside straight	Straight or one pair	10	38.4	21.7
Four Flush	Flush	9	35.0	19.6
Open ended straight draw	Straight	8	31.5	17.4
Three of kind	Full House	7	27.8	15.2
Unmatched pocket cards	Pair one	6	24.1	13.0
One matched pocket card	Two pair or Three of kind	5	20.4	10.9
Two Pair	Full House	4	16.5	8.7
Inside Straight	Straight	4	16.5	8.7
One matched pocket card	Two pair	3	12.5	6.5
Pocket Pair	Three of kind	2	8.4	4.3
Three of kind	Four of kind	1	4.3	2.2

Minimum Pot Size

A more useful way to think about drawing hands is to examine the minimum amount of winnings needed to justify the cost of continued play. The tables on the next page show for the number of available outs, the minimum pot size that must be won to justify the cost. If you cannot win the minimum amount shown in the table under the cost column, your bet is not getting the correct pot odds.

There are two tables, one for two cards to come and the other when there is one card to come. For example, playing $3-6 Hold'em, you are on a flush draw (9 outs) with two cards to come. There is a $6 bet to call and you expect to spend $12 total to get to the river. In the table for two cards to come, the intersection of the $12 column and 9 out row shows $34. You must win at least $34 to justify spending $12, because in this situation, you will have about two failures for every success.

For higher betting limits, multiply the dollar amounts by 10. Example: In a $5-10 game, you are on an inside straight draw (4 outs) and must call a raise ($20) to see the last card. In the table for one card to come, think of the $2 column as the column for $20. The value in the row for 4 outs is multiplied by 10 to give $230. You must win at least $230 to justify a $20 bet on an inside straight draw.

These tables are especially useful for Internet competition, because pot sizes are precisely displayed on your screen and the table can be in front of you for reference.

Minimum Pot Size for Correct Pot Odds

For your bets (costs for additional cards) to have correct pot odds, you must win at least the amount shown under the cost column, in the row with the number of outs available to make your hand.

ONE CARD TO COME

Outs	Cost of Final Card									
	$1	$2	$3	$4	$5	$6	$8	$10	$12	$15
1	$46	$92	$138	$184	$230	$276	$368	$460	$552	$690
2	$23	$46	$69	$92	$115	$138	$184	$230	$276	$345
3	$15	$31	$46	$61	$77	$92	$123	$153	$184	$230
4	$12	$23	$35	$46	$58	$69	$92	$115	$138	$173
5	$9	$18	$28	$37	$46	$55	$74	$92	$110	$138
6	$8	$15	$23	$31	$38	$46	$61	$77	$92	$115
7	$7	$13	$20	$26	$33	$39	$53	$66	$79	$99
8	$6	$12	$17	$23	$29	$35	$46	$58	$69	$86
9	$5	$10	$15	$20	$26	$31	$41	$51	$61	$77
10	$5	$9	$14	$18	$23	$28	$37	$46	$55	$69

TWO CARDS TO COME

Outs	Cost of Final Two Cards									
	$1	$2	$3	$4	$5	$6	$8	$10	$12	$15
1	$23	$47	$70	$93	$116	$140	$186	$233	$279	$349
2	$12	$24	$36	$48	$60	$71	$95	$119	$143	$179
3	$8	$16	$24	$32	$40	$48	$64	$80	$96	$120
4	$6	$12	$18	$24	$30	$36	$48	$61	$73	$91
5	$5	$10	$15	$20	$25	$29	$39	$49	$59	$74
6	$4	$8	$12	$17	$21	$25	$33	$41	$50	$62
7	$4	$7	$11	$14	$18	$22	$29	$36	$43	$54
8	$3	$6	$10	$13	$16	$19	$25	$32	$38	$48
9	$3	$6	$9	$11	$14	$17	$23	$29	$34	$43
10	$3	$5	$8	$10	$13	$16	$21	$26	$31	$39

Opponents' Playing Styles

Playing styles have a big influence on how each player will choose to act in a hand. Playing styles generally fall into one of the following four categories:

Loose-passive players are free with their money, but their actions tend to follow the other players. Loose-passive players enter most hands and call just about every bet, but they rarely bet or raise on their own. Generally, these players are the most profitable people to play against. Beware though, since they play every hand, potentially they can have any hand. It's difficult to know the cards they are playing. While most of their hands are weak, they can surprise you. If the table is full of loose-passive players you can play weaker starting cards since you don't have to worry about pre-flop raises and many players will be in each hand.

Loose-aggressive players are also free with money, but they thrive on action and want to be the center of attention. Loose-aggressive players raise often, even with weak cards. If they act after you, make sure you have a strong hand that justifies calling their expected raise. It's not their hand you have to worry about beating, but other players with strong cards that call their raises. Loose-aggressive players lose lots of money, but if too many of them are at a table, the entire game becomes loose-aggressive. In such a game, there are many pre-flop raises and large pots contested by many players with the flimsiest of hands. Only play with strong starting cards that justify a large pre-flop expense. Against these players, you'll have large swings in your bankroll, but you don't have to win many pots to come out ahead.

Tight-passive players are followers at the table, but very careful with their money. Tight-passive players typically buy in for a small amount of money and guard it. They seldom bet, rarely raise, and call bets only when they have a great hand. You won't lose money at a table full of these kinds of players, but it's difficult to make much, either.

When tight-passive players dominate the table, pots are smaller because few players enter each hand and there are few showdowns. To win money, you need to win many small pots by being aggressive. Bet and raise with marginal cards to intimidate these players out of the hand.

Tight-aggressive players are careful with their money, but when they do play, they seize the initiative. Tight-aggressive players enter few hands, but when they do, they have strong cards. They bet and raise aggressively, forcing the other players to pay dearly if they decide to chase. If you find yourself at a table filled with tight-aggressive players, you should consider switching to another table, especially if you are new to poker. It is easy to find yourself outplayed and your money quickly gone in this kind of game. Study the play of tight-aggressive players since you should aspire to be one.

The playing style of each person at the table influences the personality of the table as a whole. The personality of the table is important early in a hand, especially when deciding whether or not to see the flop. As the hand progresses and fewer players remain, individual personalities become more important. You need to note both the group personality (when entering a hand) and the personality of the individuals (when you go up against opponents one-on-one).

Being sensitive to playing styles and how they can change is critical. Group dynamics change as players come and go, and sometimes change for no reason at all. Tight-passive tables can suddenly become loose-aggressive tables for no apparent reason. Learning to adjust your play based on your opponents' playing styles and the group dynamics is the essence of the poker strategy described in Chapter 6.

5. Tactics

This section presents tactical plays for each stage of a hand, and provides scenarios that illustrate the best decision for commonly encountered situations. The reasons for each "best play" are explained. While working though each scenario:

• Reference the earlier chapters as needed. Each scenario uses information and terminology that has been introduced throughout the book.
• Get a deck of cards and lay out each play. The ability to visualize the potential hand that you have—and the hands that your opponents can have—is important.

Entering the Hand

After receiving pocket cards, you are immediately faced with a choice: play your cards and call the blinds, or fold. In making this choice, discipline yourself to:

• Play high cards.
• Play cards appropriate for your position.

As shown in the previous chapter, the majority of starting hands should be folded. Because premium and strong hands are rare and unevenly distributed, patience is required. You may play for two hours receiving garbage or you may get several premium hands in a row. It is important to develop the discipline to play the best cards, which at times requires long periods of waiting. Be wary of playing hands that seem stronger than they are. Having suited cards adds strength to your starting hand, but not as much as you might think. Flushes are rare hands, even when you start with two-suited cards. Much of the money won in Hold'em comes from matching a high pocket card with a high card on the board to form a high pair, in combination with a high kicker.

Remember that before the flop, checking is not an option. To see the flop, you must call at least the big blind. Raises before the flop add to your cost and usually indicate the raiser has a strong hand. Only call raises before the flop if you have a strong or premium hand. If you call the blind with a with a drawing hand in an early position, you are making yourself vulnerable to later pre-flop raises that should not be called.

When you have a premium hand, you should raise regardless of your position at the table. With AA and KK, you should re-raise. Raising from an early position tends to narrow the field and make it more likely your premium starting cards will win. Raising from a late position tends to build the pot since players who already called are less likely to fold. Your premium cards are less likely to hold up against many players, but you will win more money when they do. In either case, you benefit from raising.

With many players in the hand, you can play weaker starting cards. Drawing hands face long odds on winning, but if enough players contribute to the pot, the potential winnings make entering with a drawing hand worthwhile. For example, if you are in the last position and you have a connected straight flush draw like 5♣ 6♣, and all the other players have called but not raised the blind, entering is worthwhile. If the flop comes up 4♠ 7♦ 8♣, you have a well-disguised straight and could win big if the people holding high cards bet heavily. But the odds of hitting a flop that favorable are low. Therefore, if there are bets from the early position players and folds from the mid-position player (which leaves only 3 or 4 players), you should fold as well. The people who called in an early position have good cards and you will not win enough money in this situation to justify playing for a long shot draw.

When more players stay in the hand, or when there are more bets and raises, the pot gets large early in the hand. Large pots tend to protect themselves since players are less likely to fold when a great amount of money is on the table. When the pot is large, you should have premium starting cards or a draw to straight or Ace-high flush. Again, for small pots, drawing hands should not be played since they don't win often.

Consider the following scenarios:

Scenario 1—You are dealt 2♦ 5♣ and fold the hand following the advice to play only high cards. The flop is 2♣ 5♥ 5 ♦. Betting is heavy after the turn and river cards (10♣, J♦) and a large pot is awarded to someone holding pocket Queens. Your 5's full would have easily beat Queens and fives if you had stayed in the hand.

Don't regret your choice to fold a hand that would have been a full house: you made the correct decision. A miracle flop does not over-ride the fact that over the long run, playing low cards will cost you more money than you will win. Even your miracle flop is vulnerable to overcards on the turn or river. Had a Queen hit, the person with pocket Queens would beat you. You would also lose to opponents holding Jacks, 10's, or even 10, 5. While it is true that any two cards can win, to play profitable Hold'em, you must play high cards and fold low ones.

Scenario 2—You are dealt 10♣ J♣ and you are in an early position—to the left of the big blind. You call, and the player to your left raises. The next five people fold, and the player in the dealer position calls the raise. Then the blinds fold. Not wanting to fold after putting money in the pot, you call the raise. The flop is A♦ 2♥ 7♠. There is a bet after the flop and you fold since your hand is now worthless. You need to catch two perfect cards to make the straight.

You should have folded after the first raise. It costs too much to play for a straight or a flush in an early position, and against so few people, little money is won even if you hit your draw. The person who raised probably has a big pocket pair so you are an underdog from the start. Had you known about the raise and the small number of players, you never would have called the blind. From an early position, you can't know, so don't call.

Summary of Pre-flop Play

These scenarios illustrate wishful thinking that you need to avoid. In short:
- Play premium hands from all positions. Raise, and call raises to stay in the game until the flop. With AA and KK, re-raise.
- Play strong hands from middle and late positions. Call the big blind, but use your judgment on calling raises.
- Play drawing hands from late positions. Only call the big blind if a large number of players remain (5 or more). Use judgment on calling raises, and remember that if many people also call the raise, it is correct to stay in the hand.
- Fold all other hands.

After the Flop

After the flop, you know five of the seven cards that will form your hand. Because three of these five are community cards, the person holding the best hand after the flop is a heavy favorite to win. It is much harder to out-draw someone in Hold'em than in other forms of poker. The cards that follow the flop may improve your hand, but often they will improve the strongest hand even more. Immediately after the flop, the questions you should ask are:

- Do I have the best hand so far?
- What cards are needed to make my hand the best?
- Why are my opponents still playing?
- What cards are my opponents looking for?

Answering these questions requires the skill of "reading the flop." Consider the following categories of flops:

Flops with scare cards (Aces and face cards). A face card is King, Queen, or Jack. Because people play Aces and face cards in Hold'em, a flop with these cards usually means someone has at least one pair. Therefore the term "scare" card, when an Ace or face card appears on the board. A person who raised before the flop might well have a big pair or Ace-face in the pocket. After a flop with scare cards, that player might have trips or two pair. To continue playing after such a flop, you should have at least the top pair and a high kicker. For example, with a flop of Q, J, 7, you should hold a Queen with another Ace or face card to keep playing.

Flops with garbage cards. A flop with low cards is less likely to have paired someone. When the flop is 2♣ 5♥ 7♦, people holding high pairs and high cards in the pocket have a great advantage since it is unlikely the flop has helped anyone. Beware, though, of players in the blind who have not called a raise to see the flop. The blind's two cards could be anything since at this point the blind is not in the hand by choice. If a blind gets excited by a flop of little cards, their hand could be two pair or better. Don't underestimate their strength.

Flops with pairs. To win when this type of flop appears, you usually need to form another pair higher than the one on the board. If the flop is 10♥ 10♣ 3♠, and you hold A♣ 3♣, your two pair is not going to win without improvement. You need to pair your Ace. Everyone has a pair of tens so anyone with another pair higher than your threes beats you. Also, anytime there is a pair on the flop, it is possible for someone to have a full house. This becomes more likely when there are high cards on the board. A flop of Q♣ Q♠ J♥ is more likely to have made a full house for someone than 5♣ 5♥ 8♦.

Drawing flops. Contain matched suits and cards in (or close to) sequence. This type of flop allows for the creation of straights and flushes. Learn to recognize when they're present and when they're not. Any flop containing two cards of the same suit will attract players holding two cards of that suit since they have a 33% chance of making the flush by the end. Flops with connected cards attract people looking to draw to a straight.

Flops that allow pat hands. Flops such as three of the same suit or three connected cards, should not to be played against unless you can make the flush or the high end of the straight. If there is substantial betting and raising, someone already has the hand or a good draw, and you should fold.

Combination flops. These flops allow the formation of a variety of monster hands. Consider K♦ K♠ Q♦. If many players are holding face cards, many monster hands could result from later cards. An Ace-high or King-high straight, Diamond flush, Kings-full, Queens-full, even a royal flush could occur in this case. If you are holding Q♠ J♣, and there is substantial betting, get out. Your two pair has little chance of improving and many ways to lose.

With practice and observation, you will learn to read flops and to judge the kinds of hands your opponents are playing. Consider these scenarios:

Scenario 3—You hold A♦ Q♥ and are in a late position. The flop is Q♣ 7♦ 3♠ and the action is checked around the table to you. You are hesitant to bet since you only have a pair of Queens.

Your pair of Queens with an Ace kicker is probably the best hand at this point and should be bet. Additional cards stand a better chance of improving your hand more than your opponents' hands. For example, if an Ace appears, an opponent holding A, K has a pair of Aces, but you'll have Aces and Queens. Another Queen gives you trip-Queens. If a 7 appears, an opponent holding a pair of Jacks has Jacks and 7's, but you still win with Queen's and 7's. There are ways for you to lose: someone might have a pair of 7's in the pocket, but they would have bet them ahead of you. Most likely you have the best hand, and you should bet accordingly.

Scenario 4—You hold 6♦ 7♦ and are in a late position. You and six other players are competing for the pot. The flop comes 8♠ 9♠ 10♥. There is a bet ahead of you, a raise, and someone calls that raise. Excited about your straight, you call the raise.

You should have folded. With this many players betting and raising, someone already has a higher straight (like a Jack, Queen), and the players that call are on a flush draw or holding King - Queen and hoping for a Jack on the board to make a King-high straight. Your hand is already second best and can never improve. Remember that people play the high cards in Hold'em. Time to get out.

Summary of Post-flop Play

- Unless you have the best hand, or a draw to the best hand, you should not invest additional money after the flop.
- Knowing when a mediocre hand is the best and should be bet, and knowing when a strong hand is second best and needs to be folded, is the hallmark of a good poker player.

After the Turn

After the turn, bets double. Your judgment of opponents and the pot odds dictate when you should stay in the hand.

- Learn to put your opponents on a hand and play accordingly.
- Invest your money in proportion to the size of the pot.

When your opponents are on the draw against you, betting to protect your hand is necessary, even when they have the correct pot odds to call your bets. Many beginning poker players fall into the trap of not betting their good hands (thinking that this would alert their opponents that they have a good hand) and calling with weak hands in hopes of catching a winning card. This is the exact opposite of what should be done. When you have the best hand, you must bet and force the other players to pay to draw you out. Letting them see additional cards without calling a bet is giving them free cards—the equivalent of giving them infinite pot odds. You must force opponents to make decisions. Don't worry about concealing the strength of your hand. You win more money betting with good cards because opponents learn to respect your bets and fold their marginal hands. You might win a showdown with a strong hand, but you always win when your opponents fold, no matter what your cards are.

Sometimes, when many players are contesting the pot, it is not correct to bet with the best hand. If many people are on a draw to beat you, the odds are that at least one of them will. This situation is known as *implied collusion*. If, for practical purposes, your opponents are colluding against you, it is better to stay in the hand as cheaply as possible. Implied collusion occurs most often when the pot is large from the beginning (many people called pre-flop raises) and everyone has the correct pot odds to stay, no matter how great the odds against their draw.

When you are on a draw, there are cases when it is correct to call bets when the pot is small, provided that the size of the pot you expect to win is large enough to justify calling the bet. In this case, you are basing your decision to play on *implied pot odds*—the ratio of the expected money in the pot against the cost to play. Estimating the implied odds requires you to judge your opponents' behavior and intentions. For example, in a small-pot game where you expect additional callers later on or in an additional round of betting, it is correct for you to call as well.

These following scenarios illustrate the importance of playing pot odds to your advantage.

Scenario 5—You hold A♣ J♠ and the flop is A♦ J♦ 3♣. You bet and everyone folds, except for one player who you suspect is on a flush draw. The turn card is 5♠, and she checks to you. Worried that the last card might be the diamond she needs, you check. The last card is indeed a diamond. She bets; you call. A showdown confirms her to have a flush.

You saved money on this hand by not betting your two pair at the turn, but you made a terrible play. Your opponent paid nothing to draw to her flush. She got a free card since she had nothing to lose by staying in the hand. Four out of five times (80%), she will not hit the flush and you win the hand. You must make her pay to beat you. Over the long run, you will win much more money than you lose.

Scenario 6—You hold A♣ 9♣ in a late position and the flop is 5♣ 8♣ K♦. There is a bet and seven callers including you. At the turn, a Q♠ appears. A bet is followed by a raise that six people call. The pot is now over $100, and you need to call a $12 bet to stay in. You hesitate, knowing that 80% of the time you will not make your flush.

Because of the large pot, you must call this bet. In this situation, you may win only one out of five tries, but the one $100 win is greater than the $60 cost of making this play five times. Over the long run, you will come out ahead. Your opponents are correct in making you pay to beat them, but you are correct in calling. However, if the pot contained only $40, your best play is to fold because the amount you win doesn't justify the cost.

Summary of Play After the Turn

• If you have the best hand, make people pay to beat you.
• If you are on a draw, make sure the pot size justifies the cost.

At the River

All the cards are out. At this point you want to:

• Get the maximum value from your winning hands.
• Minimize your losses to opponents who have outdrawn you.

If you led throughout the hand, meaning you always bet and the others called, keep betting unless a scare card appears (an overcard to your hand or a card that appears to complete someone else's straight or flush). If this happens, check. You do not want your bet raised by someone who has outdrawn you. Use your judgment on calling bets. If your opponent only bets on the end with the best hand, don't throw money away to "keep him honest." Money saved is money won. Sometimes in the last round of betting, you know exactly how you stand. If you have the nuts, bet or if possible, raise. If you missed a draw, cut your losses and fold.

An inevitable part of poker is the *bad beat*. You have the best hand all the way. Only one or two cards in the deck can beat you and at the river, one of them appears. Most often this happens when someone keeps a little pair in the pocket (such as 3, 3) and calls all your bets and raises on your top two pair (even though they do not have the correct pot odds). At the river a 3 appears, a card that looks harmless but beats you. Nothing can be done about bad beats. You cannot hesitate to bet when you have a strong hand, nor can you start playing for improbable draws yourself. Bad beats are part of the normal statistical fluctuations in the game. Your play must be geared towards the long-term trends, not the fluctuations.

Scenario 7—You are in an early position holding A♣ 10♦, and the board is K♣ Q♠ J♣ 3♦ 7♥. You hold the nuts. Your Ace-high straight cannot be beat since no flushes or boats can be formed from this board. Not wanting to scare people out of the pot, you check and then everyone else checks as well. You win at showdown.

It is rarely correct to check with the nuts. You should usually bet. If no one calls, it is the same result as everyone checking. By betting, you force your opponents to make decisions. Give your opponents opportunities to make mistakes.

Scenario 8—You are in an early position, holding Q♣, J♦, and at the turn, the board is 3♣ Q♦ J♣ 3♥. You bet and one player calls. The river card is an A♣. You bet again but this time your opponent raises. You call the raise and find that your opponent held A♦ K♥. Your Queens and Jacks loses to Aces and threes.

The appearance of an overcard on the river should make you cautious, especially when the card is an Ace or King. People tend to hold on to Aces and Kings. In this situation, anyone holding an Ace beats you. Always ask yourself why your opponent is staying for the river card. For this board, the A♦ K♥ hand had ten outs. If any of the three remaining Aces, three remaining Kings, or four remaining 10's appears at the river, you lose.

Summary of Play at the River

- If you have the best hand, bet. Make your opponents pay.
- If you missed a draw or know your opponent made their draw, fold. Money saved is money won.

Deception

Pure *bluffing*—betting heavily with a garbage hand all the way to the river—rarely works in poker. To get away with a pure bluff, you need to establish yourself as a tight-aggressive player and play opponents who, observing that, respect your bets. Even then, pure bluffing won't work against someone with the nuts. Of course, one reason for bluffing is to get caught occasionally, which deceives opponents into calling your future bets on strong hands. However, in low-limit Hold'em games, which are mostly populated by loose-passive players, you will have callers whether you bluff or not. That makes excessive use of bluffing costly since you will lose when you bluff, and it is not necessary to deceive people since your strong hands will be called anyway. Even without pure bluffing, there are many ways to practice deception. Consider these scenarios.

Scenario 9—You hold A♣ 9♣ in a late position and the flop is Q♣ Q♥ 10♣. There is an early position bet; three people call and you raise. Everyone after you folds except the players already in the hand, who call the raise. The turn card is A♦; everyone checks to you and you check. The river card is an 8♣ completing your flush. Everyone again checks; you bet and there is one caller—the player who first bet who holds K♥ Q♦. Your flush beats the trip Queens.

Your raise was a *semi-bluff* since your hand was not the best but had a good chance of improving. The raise did several things. It bought a free card since the player with the best hand after the flop (trip Queens), fearing your raise, never bet them again. By inducing your opponents to check, you saw the river card for free. Since bets double after the turn, your raise was only half the amount required to call a bet after the turn card (a significant savings). Your raise also provided information. Your opponent could have flopped a full house and you could be *drawing dead*—that is, even if you hit the flush, you still lose. Not re-raising, and checking to you later on, is a signal that your opponent does not have a full house or four of a kind.

Scenario 10—You hold K♣ Q♦ in a mid-position. The flop is J♣, 10♥, 7♠, and the action is checked to you. With an open-ended straight draw, but nothing else, you bet. The next player raises, one other player calls the raise, everyone else folds, and you call the raise. The turn card is a 9♠, giving you the nut straight. It is your turn but you check, feigning fear over the raise and the straight possibility on the board. The player who raised previously bets and is called by the remaining player and then yourself. The river card is a 3♣, giving you the nuts. You check again; there is a bet; the other player folds; then you raise. Your opponent, the original raiser, who holds J♥ J♣, feels obliged to call.

Your deceptive play in this hand won a great deal of money. Had you checked your straight draw, and bet when the straight possibility appeared on the board, your opponent with the trip Jacks would have been more careful at the end. By doing the reverse, you trained your opponent to bet for you and were able to execute a successful check-raise on the end. Your opponents will also be wary in the future and not automatically take a check as a sign of weakness. It is usually a bad play to check with the nuts on the river, but this play worked because your opponent had a strong hand (as indicated by the raise) and you deceived him into believing it to be the best hand.

It is not correct to always play drawing hands in a deceptive manner. Often you will check when drawing, and bet when you hit the draw. However, these are ways to vary your play, and keep opponents off balance. Making intentionally misleading plays does assume your opponents are skilled and think about their actions. Opponents who don't think cannot be deceived. Against opponents who call no matter what, don't make fancy deceptive plays—they won't notice. When your opponents call all the time the only way to win is to have the best cards at the end.

6. Strategies

For successful play, it is necessary to have knowledge of the mathematical facts and tactical plays described in the previous sections. That knowledge alone will not make you successful. Your play must have an underlying strategy, a broad plan that provides a context for each action. This section discusses strategic considerations. Interwoven through this discussion are what I call "life analogies," which are a series of behavioral examples from life that illustrate poker concepts. Dan Kimberg in his book *Serious Poker*, makes the astute observation that while most sports professionals believe their sport is a metaphor for life, "poker players believe the converse—that life is a metaphor for poker."*

It helps to first consider why there is no magic formula for winning at poker. Imagine a formula exists that does win at poker. A formula means a pre-determined set of actions for all situations encountered. In situation 1, do A, in situation 2, do B, and so on. Once the formula is known, it would immediately become useless because poker is a zero-sum game. One person's loss is another one's gain. If everybody plays the exact same way, over time the cards are evenly distributed so all the situations encountered become equally distributed. The result is that no one has an advantage, money flows back and forth without accumulating for any one person.

To win at poker, your actions must be different from the other players, different in a way that gives you the edge.

* Dan Kimberg, *Serious Poker,* 2nd Edition (ConJelCo, Pittsburgh, PA, 2002) page 2.

Clearly, a winning poker strategy must be a dynamic one—that is, a strategy that continually adjusts to conditions. The strategy outlined is based on the five decision factors described in Chapter 4: your cards, position, cost, number of players, and opponents' playing style, combined with a classification of game conditions that are described next. The premise of the strategy is that the weight given to each decision factor depends on the game conditions. For example, your position under some game conditions is not an important factor. In a different set of game conditions position becomes the most important factor.

To classify game conditions, four extreme cases are identified and the strategic considerations appropriate for each discussed. A given poker game usually does not precisely match one of the extremes, but often a game will have enough elements of one of the extreme cases that knowing what to do in the extreme, provides a good strategic starting point.

Life Analogy – Investing

Over the long run, investing in the market is *not* a zero-sum game. Historically, wealth and the living standards that go with wealth tend to increase over time. By investing in funds that track the general market, it is possible to have a share in the expanding economy and accumulate money over time.

However, the dream of most investors is to "beat the market"—that is, to make more money than the market as a whole by buying and selling securities from other investors in such a way that money flows from them to us. Can there be a magic formula for beating the market? Obviously not or we would all apply the formula and be multimillionaires overnight. That cannot happen because in the short term, investing is a zero-sum game: over a short period of time there is only a finite amount of money available.

To beat the market, it is necessary to become educated about the securities being traded. Over the last decade, the Internet has made it possible for all investors to know more about the securities they trade. With a computer and Internet access, a click of a mouse makes it possible to know company financials, breaking news, real-time prices, and make immediate purchases. However, all this information has not made it easier to beat the market. When everyone has access to the same information, any change that occurs is reflected immediately in the price. Prices moved in an orderly fashion a few decades ago as information on a company slowly filtered to investors. Today prices move abruptly overnight or in minutes, when thousands of investors respond to breaking news posted on the Internet.

Has the explosion of information, fast trade executions, and technical stock charts made it easier to beat the market? No, it has not. Many people may claim otherwise, but look around. How many people do you know who are quitting their jobs to become securities traders? Today investors are more knowledgeable, but beating the market is still as difficult as ever because for the most part, everyone has equal access to the same information. No matter how much information is available, when it is equally shared, no one has an edge.

There are people who do beat the market because they make better decisions. But the adjective "better" means their decisions are also different from the majority. Their decisions cannot be part of a formula, but must adjust to changes in the market before the change happens. Usually, people who are successful at beating the market have a talent for making adjustments ahead of time. They anticipate the next big trend before the crowd starts the stampede.

Classifying Game Characteristics

In Chapter 4, individual playing styles were classified into four broad groups: loose-passive, loose-aggressive, tight-passive, and tight-aggressive. Poker games themselves also fit into these categories. In attaching an adjective to a poker game, it is the general behavior of the group being described. How does a group of people playing a game together take on a style of it own? It happens in much the same way that the individuals acquire their playing styles: It depends on the underlying reasons for the game.

The object of poker is to win money, but that is not the only reason for the game. Often, winning money isn't even the most important reason for the game. In Alan N. Schoonmaker's book, *The Psychology of Poker,* he explains that we are kidding ourselves if we think poker is only about money. For all but a few professionals, poker is a game, not a job.

People play games for many reasons: competition, socializing, entertainment, mental challenge, etc. Money is rarely the primary motive. In fact, compared to the expense of some games, such as golf or yacht racing, a person could lose money consistently in low-limit poker games, have a good time, and still be better off financially. Some people have this view of poker—that they are paying for entertainment.

To formulate a correct strategy, you need to examine the underlying reasons for the game in which you choose to play. Two reasons must be considered in the most detail. (1) Money is a meaningful component to a poker game. It is how the game is scored, but the relative importance of money to the players must be weighed. In many situations, no one cares that much about the money. (2) Just as important as money is the social question—are people playing for friendly entertainment or for hard-nosed competition?

Imagine a two-dimensional grid where on the horizontal scale, the importance of money is plotted, and on the vertical scale is the degree of competitiveness. The next figure illustrates the grid. As games increase in competitiveness, their character changes from passive to aggressive. As money increases in importance, the game changes from loose to tight. The four corners of the grid are the extremes. The four poker situations that best exemplify the four extremes and the appropriate strategy for each case are discussed. Each quadrant of the grid represents games that are closest to one of the extremes. A different one of the five decision factors becomes most critical as the nature of the game moves to different quadrants. The critical factor is the one you need to weigh the most when making decisions on your hands. The nature of the game often means that safe assumptions can be made on the other decision factors. The recommended strategy will incorporate the safe assumptions and give careful consideration to the critical factor. Also described are the common frustrations and mistakes associated with each extreme.

THE STRATEGIC GRID

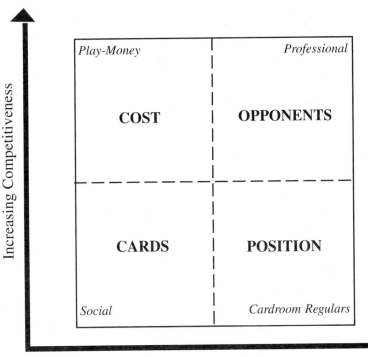

Life Analogy – Why do people work?

For the money, right? No paycheck equals no food, no housing, no clothes and none of the other necessities and luxuries that sustain our lives. At least that's the answer we give our kids who are always laying claim to our paycheck. However, money is only part of the reason we or anyone else works. Examples abound of people whose work cannot be motivated by money. There are people who work even though they don't need money. Does Bill Gates go to work because he needs money? Most heads of large companies have plenty of money and could retire early, yet they still work.

Politicians work for power, influence and a place in history. The President of the United States is paid far less than a president or CEO in private industry. Clearly the President, usually a well-off person to start with, is not motivated by the paycheck. Some people work low-paying jobs that they love when they could be working high-paying jobs that interest them less. Many artists and musicians fall into this category; their urge to create outweighs their desire for money.

People also take pride in their work. Along with a paycheck, most of us want recognition for our efforts and expressions of appreciation. We want our boss, co-workers, and customers to say we did something important for them. Book authors, such as myself, hope to create something meaningful and influential. I hope this book will be a product that changes people in a positive way.

It is necessary for people to receive money in order to work, but it is rarely the only reason why people work.

THE FOUR EXTREME POKER GAMES

Social—a loose-passive game. A game played for entertainment.
Play money—a loose-aggressive game. A game played for competition.
Cardroom regulars—a tight-passive game. A game played for money and entertainment.
Professional—a tight-aggressive game. A game played for money and competition.

Loose-passive Games
(Social Poker)

Once a month I get together with the same group of friends for a night of poker. We play unstructured "dealer's choice" games. Each chip is worth a dime and bets are rarely more than 50 cents. We do not play table stakes so we are constantly fishing green out of our pockets when our chip pile runs low. However, there is an "understanding" that if your hand is a monster, you won't be throwing down 10 and 20-dollar bills. We drink beer, munch salty snacks, at the half point eat a meal of cold-cut sandwiches, talk about sports, work, the stock market, and generally have a good time. On a really bad night, I might loose $30 and on a good night, I make that amount. It always feels better to win than to loose, but if you are the loser that night, where else could you have had such a good time for so little money? On poker night, we play Hold'em and Seven-Card Stud, but we also play many junk poker games with wild cards and antes high in relation to the final pot size. In high ante games where most of money in the pot has gone in before anyone sees their cards, it is impossible to gain an edge. Since the game consists of the same seven people, playing month after month, year after year, money just flows around the circle. Over time, no one wins or loses—a perfect social situation.

The social game I play with my friends is an extreme example of a loose-passive game. The defining features of these games are few raises and everyone plays until the end. There is always a show-down. If you go to a casino cardroom on a weekend, at the lower betting limits you will find games that are close to fitting the loose-passive definition. Tourists, beginners, and people out to have a good time populate these games. Money is not the main issue—entertain-ment is the attraction. The stakes are small compared with the costs of most entertainment/social activities. Loose-passive games are ac-tually the easiest ones to beat. To win money, you must become anti-social: that is, not play every hand through to the end.

Strategic Considerations for Loose-passive Games

Primary reasons for the game—entertainment, socializing.
Money—no one cares.
Competitiveness—low.

Safe Assumptions:

Position is unimportant since everyone will call with every hand. There is little information to be gained from having an advantageous position.

Cost will be small in relation to the pot. Just about every drawing hand will have decent pot odds.

Number of players equals the number in the group. Everyone plays every hand.

Playing styles are passive. People rarely raise, even with the nuts.

Most Important Factor:

Your Cards. The only way to get an edge is to do what the others will not: fold unproductive hands.

Frustrating Features of Loose-passive Games:

Bad beats. After a long session of play where you end just about even, you will be thinking about the several hundred dollars sitting on the table that you still consider yours. Of course, the money is not yours because of that one last improbable card on the end that beat you. With so many people staying to the end in each hand, implied collusion is rampant. Bad beats are an unavoidable cost of play.

Putting people on hands. When there are six hands up against you, how do you figure out what they all are? Someone is on a straight draw; someone is on a flush draw; someone flopped two-pair; someone has a small pocket pair and is waiting for a set. But which one of your opponents is in each of these situations?

A Common Mistake:

Over aggression, particularly raising after the flop. You flop a flush draw; a person in front of you bets. How strong is their hand? You raise to find out and expect that you will also get a free card. Three players after you call your raise and so does the original bettor. You have learned nothing, and with this many players, odds are that you will not get your free card. Often it is better to get your flush draw as cheaply as possible and worry about raising if you do hit the flush because someone will still call at the end.

Strategy:

Fold frequently. If you watch the game and see ten hands in a row ending with a showdown, will that change with your presence? If no one's bets are respected, yours will not be either. To claim the pot, you must have the best cards at showdown. Forget about bluffing— it won't work. What you can be loose on in these games is the position requirement for your starting cards. You can play drawing hands from an early position because you can safely assume that the requirements for playing a drawing hand—large pot, no pre-flop raise—will always be present.

However, don't start playing garbage for starting cards and think that, because there are always many callers, anything is playable. Playing garbage is a seductive trap in loose-passive games because any two starting cards can hit the flop and win a big pot. All the pots are big, so don't compete unless you have an edge at the beginning. One way to think about loose-passive games is to imagine a poker player's dream where every hand has a large pot and you are always dealt the best starting cards. Want to realize that dream? Then fold every garbage hand that comes your way. With correct strategy, loose-passive games are the most profitable to play in.

Loose-aggressive Games
(Play-money Poker)

Go onto the Internet and join one of the play-money games. You will find poker play at its most aggressive—raising wars with raises frequently capped, people betting heavily on the flimsiest of cards, and no caution shown when scary cards appear on the board. Of course, everyone can afford to be aggressive because the money is truly meaningless—there isn't any. Play-money poker is an extreme example of a loose-aggressive game. The defining features are a lot of betting and raising with little consideration of the cards. Loose-aggressive players are there for the competition. They are also the people who like to gamble.

Play-money poker is a good approximation of loose-aggressive games, because for loose-aggressive players, money is something they *play* with. Part of the thrill is unnerving the other players with their lack of caution towards money. Often it only takes one or two loose-aggressive players to turn an entire table into loose-aggressive play. Everyone starts throwing money around to show that the aggressive player does not intimidate them. Soon the whole table is on a tilt.

Strategic Considerations for Loose-aggressive Games

Primary reasons for the game—entertainment, competition.
Money—no one cares.
Competitiveness—high.

Safe Assumptions:

Your Cards. You will always pay dearly to get to the river in loose-aggressive games. Often you will pay dearly just to see the flop. Make sure your cards are worth it. If you wouldn't raise with the cards you have, don't call because you should assume that someone will raise later on.

Position is important but in a different way. What counts is your seat in relation to the aggressive players. Many poker books will advise you to sit so that aggressive players are on your right, meaning that they act before you do. By acting after an aggressive player, you have better knowledge of the cost to play your cards. If the aggressive player stays in the hand, fold all but your strongest cards because it will cost too much to play speculative hands. While this is true, in my experience, there are also advantages to having loose-aggressive players on your left and having them act after you. Assume from the beginning that the aggressive player will bet and only play your strong cards. But only bet those strong cards if you have to. In most cases, hold back and let the aggressive player bet for you. Check when it's your turn and either call or raise the bet when the action comes back. The other players will often pay to chase a loose-aggressive player when they would not pay to chase you.

Number of players. Usually, more than half the players will see the flop no matter how many pre-flop raises there are. Often, raises will goad loose-aggressive players into staying in the hand rather than drive them out. The more action, the more they feel compelled to play. They hate being left out.

Playing styles are aggressive. Plan on calling raises before and after the flop. Seeing the river card will always be expensive. Big money will be wagered by the other players on marginal and speculative hands.

Most Important Factor:

Cost. Make sure you are getting the correct pot odds when you throw your money out. There will be a constant temptation to gamble. In some situations, it will be correct to gamble because there will be so much money on the table that any draw is playable. Other times, the same draw should be folded because the money at stake is too small.

Frustrating Features of Loose-aggressive Games:

Making sense of your opponents. There may not be any rationale behind their play so don't think too hard about their thought processes.

Wild swings in your bankroll. Loose games always result in bad beats. Add aggression to the mix and you get costly bad beats. When you do win, the pot is large, but it takes painful losses along the way to the winnings. The result is wild swings in your bankroll. It becomes tempting to not want to leave the table unless you've had an upswing, and then you still don't want to leave because it is an upswing. Loose-aggressive games require disciplined play.

A Common Mistake:

Getting caught up in pre-flop raising wars while holding mediocre pocket cards. This is especially seductive when you are one of the blinds. Any time someone is in a blind position, they feel they already paid to see the flop and should do so no matter what. Blinds are a cost of play and yes, occasionally, you get lucky and with a pair of garbage cards for a blind, hit a great flop. But don't call one or two raises in the blind when with those same two cards, you would not pay anything to see the flop. Learn to let your blind money go, and don't feel you have to chase it.

Strategy:

Pay close attention to the pot odds. The pot size varies greatly from hand to hand in loose-aggressive games. For a large pot, it may be correct to call two raises if you are on a draw, especially if four or five others call, too. However, for the exact same draw and a small pot, calling raises could cost too much. It requires great discipline to know when the same situation with the cards is a different betting situation because of the pot odds. There is a tendency for people to play the same cards the same way.

Consider an inside straight draw. You might adhere to the adage "never draw to an inside straight" and always fold, or you might be a player who never folds any kind of draw, including one to an inside straight. However, correct strategy requires a cold mathematical evaluation of the pot odds. The chart in Chapter 4 shows that with one card to come on a draw with four outs, such as an inside straight, there is an 8.7% chance of success. In a $3–6 game, if every time you draw to an inside straight it costs $6 to see the final card, you will spend an average of $70 for each success. That means every time you try this play, there must be at least $70 in the pot or over the long-run you will not turn a profit. In a tight $3–6 game, there rarely is this much money in the pot and folding is almost always the correct play. But in a loose-aggressive $3–6 game, pots will easily exceed $70 if all the players at the table call a pre-flop raise. When the pot is that large and you have an inside straight draw, you *must* make the bet.

Maintaining cost discipline is psychologically difficult, because of normal statistical fluctuations and the fact that in Hold'em, unlike other forms of poker, you get to see what your last card would have been if you had not folded. What this means is that there will be times when folded hands would have won and hands you stayed with lose and you will know in each case. Don't change your strategy because of these normal statistical fluctuations. Over the long run, it will cost you money if you leave big pots on the table unchallenged because you refuse to draw to an inside straight, or insist on always drawing, even with small pots, just in case the right card comes up.

Tight-passive Games
(Cardroom Regulars)

Visit a St. Louis Riverboat or a cardroom in suburban Seattle in the middle of the day, in the middle of the week, and you will encounter tables filled with "regulars." A "regular" means someone who plays in the same cardroom several times a week, each week. These people are easy to recognize. The employees greet them by name when they arrive and even comment on their arrival time as being either late, on-time, or early. They chat with dealers and each other in a manner that assumes a shared history. You would have to know about cardroom events from the last month to understand half the conversations. At the table, there are five sets of eyes sizing up you and your play. They are clearly studying you and not each other. The scrutiny can be unnerving, although it means that they don't know you at first (an advantage) and learning about them is easier since the familiar ways in which they treat each other conveys information.

Games filled with regulars have much in common with social home games. The players are there to pass the time, playing a game they all love, in a relaxed, friendly atmosphere. The key difference is that the money is meaningful. It has to be, otherwise they would not be regulars. Unlike a home poker club where the same $20 gets passed around the same group of people, the stakes in these games are higher and the house gets a cut of each hand dealt. If the players are equally matched, over time the house will accumulate all the money as it gets passed back and forth. These are not zero-sum games.

Strategic Considerations for Tight-passive Games

Primary reasons for the game—entertainment, money.
Money—little is available to win.
Competitiveness—low.

Safe Assumptions:

Cards. Players don't compete unless they have good cards. Expect that people paying to see the flop will have Aces, face cards, and pairs.

Cost. High in relation to the pot size. You rarely have the correct pot odds to chase. Chasing is a common and costly mistake in these games.

Number of players. 3–4, the two blinds and maybe one or two callers. With few hands dealt, high cards and high pairs increase in value.

Opponent's playing style. Predictable and passive. Pre-flop raises are rare and usually mean a high pair or A, K. Bluffing is rare. If you are going head-to-head at the end against someone hoping they've bluffed, you are going to lose.

Most Important Factor:

Position. Since players are predictable in these games, there is a lot of information available when you have an advantageous position. Acting after a solid player, who only bets strong cards, means that you know the strength of their cards before making a decision on your hand.

Frustrating Features of Tight-passive Games

No action on your best hands. You flop a monster boat and get no callers. Your highest ranked hands of the playing session may generate little income.

Blinds can whittle away your chip pile. Pots are so small they often don't generate enough income to replenish your blinds. A big win to get yourself firmly in the black is hard to come by. Worse, if you fall behind, it is hard to catch up.

A Common Mistake:

Becoming too tight yourself. With so little money in each pot, there is a temptation not to bet your moderate hands. It is common in these games to see head-to-head play where no bets are made. The two players check to each other while the dealer runs the rest of the cards. Their thinking is, why risk anything for such a small pot? The problem is, you will not make money with this kind of passive play. If you have a decent hand, bet.

Strategy :

Make little wins add up. The key is to counter the general passivity with careful aggression. "Careful" is a strange adjective for aggression, but you need a good poker sense to know when to be aggressive. Because the players only play good cards, unrestrained aggression will not necessarily intimidate them. But if you establish yourself as a tight player by being in few hands and showing good cards early on, whenever you sense weakness or hesitation from the opposition, go for the pot, even if it is small. You have to steal a few small pots in these kinds of games or you will never cover your blinds. Knowing how to play your position is key. It is risky to bet ahead of tight players when you have marginal cards. If you act first and bet a marginal hand and a rock solid player calls or raises, its time to fold.

However, if you hold the same marginal hand in last position and the rock solid players check to you, a bet often wins the pot outright. In both these cases your cards may be the same, but your position determines which play is profitable.

Typically in tight-passive games, there is not much money on the table. An extreme tight-passive player buys-in for the table minimum and guards the chips, putting money in the pot only when they have a lock. You cannot win money that is not in play and you certainly can't win more money than is on the table. If you see three or more players at a table behaving in this manner, consider finding another game. Your profit potential is limited and if you do fall behind, you have no hope of catching up.

Tight-aggressive Games
(Professional Poker)

For people who make a living from poker, low-limit games are not going to generate enough income. There isn't enough money on a low-limit table to live on, and you cannot win more than the available amount of money. You might think that the only difference between $2–4 Hold'em and $20–40 is the additional zero, but that is not the case. As the stakes are raised, money increases in meaning because attitudes towards money do not scale. Consider asking a middle-class person earning $50,000 per year to give you $10 and you are likely to get it. Ask a Fortune 500 CEO earning $50 million per year for the same fraction of their income, $10,000, and it is unlikely to be given to you. The greater the dollar amount, the tighter people are. That attitude change carries over into high-limit games. While many players pay to see the flop when it is only a dollar or two, behavior changes when it's a twenty dollar bill.

Strategic Considerations for Tight-aggressive Games

Primary reasons for the game—competition, money.
Money—people play to win.
Competitiveness—high.

Safe Assumptions:

Cards. Players usually have good cards, but be careful. They will mix things up and you should, too.

Position. You must play your position correctly and expect that others are doing the same.

Cost. High in relation to the pot size. Tight-aggressive players bet and raise to protect their hands. You are not allowed to limp in with mediocre cards when they have strong hands.

Number of players. 3–4, the two blinds and maybe one or two callers. Just as in tight-passive games, the fact that fewer hands are played means that high cards and high pairs stand up more often.

Most Important Factor:

Opponents' playing styles. To gain an edge you must pay close attention to the people. Tight-aggressive players have underlying reasons for their actions which on a rational level make sense. These people are not governed by their emotion of the moment like loose-aggressive players often are. If you can discern their plans and strategies, it is possible for you to gain an edge by anticipating their actions.

Frustrating Features of Tight-aggressive Games:

Players are good. It is easy to find yourself outplayed. Experience counts in tight-aggressive games. You are studying your opponents, but they are also studying you, and they might be better at discerning your actions than you are at discerning theirs.

Little room for error. A single mistake on your part can make the difference between a winning and losing session. Tight-aggressive players don't make the kind of fundamental mistakes (such as playing too many marginal hands for too long) that loose players make. There is much less money going into the pot from players who have almost no chance of winning. That means it is harder to recoup losses.

A Common Mistake:

Passivity. It is easy in these types of games to be intimidated into folding hands with which you should have stayed the course. Hands that are nearly worthless in loose-passive games because so many players are on a draw, are valuable in tight-aggressive games. Suppose you hold A,Q and the flop is Q, 5, 4, of different suits. If the next two cards match one of the suits on the board, the flush possibility might discourage you from betting in a loose-passive game with six players vying for the pot. Loose players actually play these kinds of draws. But in a tight-aggressive game, no one stays just because they are hoping for two matching cards to make a flush. If you have a top pair and top kicker in this situation, place a bet.

Strategy:

You must rethink what it means to have a good flop in a tight-aggressive game. The best flop for your cards may not be the best flop for your wallet. To illustrate this paradox, consider a time I had A,K, in a loose-aggressive game and the flop came up with three Aces. I got action on this hand because a loose-aggressive player in front of me thought he could bluff. The other players didn't believe him because he always bluffed and called his bets. I was in last position so all I had to do was quietly call to blend in with the unbelievers. This kind of play would never happen in a tight-aggressive game. If I held A, K, and the flop came up three Aces, I would have a worthless hand. No one would give me any action. To get action in a tight-aggressive game, it would be better if the flop didn't contain an Ace. A flop of K, 7, 3, would generate more action and I would still be in a good position. I would not have the lock of all the Aces, but if someone bet into me with a King, I would have the top kicker. An Ace could still fall later on and it is less likely that the 7 or the 3 are a threat, which they might be in a loose-aggressive game where people play any two cards.

Not only must you rethink what it means to have a good flop, you must also rethink what it means to have a good hand. You may get away with stealing pots by betting marginal cards, and then lose with strong cards. The difference is that your opponents won't challenge you unless they have strong cards. When your opponents are weak, they will back down. The attitude, "I'll call to keep him honest," that pervades loose games doesn't exist in tight-aggressive games. If your opponents call or raise, don't become confident just because your cards are good this hand, and in a prior hand that you won, your cards were weaker. Your strong hands may be losers if tight-aggressive players are not respecting your bets.

Life Analogy – Investment scams

In recent years, the news has been full of investment scams. All scams have a common element: to induce herd behavior and then run in the opposite direction. What makes something a scam is the element of dishonesty. Scam artists say things they know to be untrue for the purpose of profit. The direction of the stampede does not matter so long as the scam artist goes the opposite way. For example:

Pump and dump. The now-classic example is Enron. By use of phony accounting, the top executives created huge demand for their company's stock into which they sold their shares. By the time the public realized that their shares of Enron were worthless, the top executives had cashed out hundreds of millions of dollars.

Trash and stash. This is the same basic idea as a "pump and dump scam," but it is done in reverse. A notable example occurred on August 25, 2000, when a college student concocted a phony press release distributed over the Internet, stating that Emulex would not meet earnings expectations. In less than an hour, the company's share price fell 62%, wiping away $2.5 billion of market capitalization. Of course the scam artist shorted shares of Emulex prior to his hoax and covered his short position with cheap shares purchased while the sellers stampeded.

While these are extreme examples of herd behavior brought on by dishonesty, they illustrate a truth that applies to honest investment decisions. The truth is that you will never make money when you are part of a stampede. To profit, you must be standing apart from the crowd.

Analyzing Game Characteristics

To think about poker strategically is difficult. Most people play the game by looking for the right cards. They hope that their starting cards are good, that the flop hits them, that they will outdraw the other players, and that the other players will not outdraw them. Thinking never progresses beyond what cards will improve my hand, and what cards I should fear.

To go beyond the superficial analysis of cards, you need to develop the mental discipline to analyze the kind of game you are in, both before, during, and after play. While your name is on the waiting list, scope the games you might enter. During the game, think about whether the table dynamics have changed. After play, think about the key decisions you made. Keep a poker diary and analyze which plays worked and which did not.

To orient your approach to the game in terms of the strategic grid (figure on Page 73), here is a list of questions you should ask yourself while observing games:

- Are raises frequent or rare?
- Are showdowns frequent or rare?
- On average, do many players pay to see the flop, or just a few?
- On average, how large are the pots in relation to the final bet size?
- Are common drawing hands (see the charts on Page 52) getting the correct pot odds?
- Are players showing good starting cards at showdown, or just about anything?
- What is the demeanor of each player?
- Are people relaxed and socializing or serious and intense?
- What are the sizes of the chip piles?
- Does a large chip pile represent a large buy-in or a winning player?
- Does a small chip pile represent a small buy-in or a losing player?
- Do raises scare players out of the hand or egg them on?
- Are there obviously aggressive players?
- Are there obviously tight players?

For online games, the ability to take written notes means that you can be even more systematic in game analysis. When I am checking out online games, I use the chart on the next page to note the actions on at least ten hands prior to joining the game (I don't take notes while I play because it is too time-consuming). Extreme behavior is particularly revealing about the nature of the game. Does every hand end in a showdown? Are there never any pre-flop raises? Answer yes to those two questions and it is a loose-passive game. By mentally asking yourself the kinds of questions listed, you will be able to orient yourself on the strategic grid and know the critical factors in your decision-making.

Summary

Poker is an exquisitely balanced game. For every action there is a counteraction, for every strategy a counter strategy. Much like martial art that depends on balance and timing, your approach to poker must be dynamic and adjustable. In his book *The Theory of Poker,* Sklansky provides a table of common poker mistakes and corresponding strategies for exploiting each mistake.* All the mistakes are described in terms of extremes, such as bluffs too much, bluffs too little, never bluffs, never slow plays. Each mistake requires a counter strategy tailored to turn your opponents' excesses against them. The lesson I take from Sklansky's table is that poker is not a game about strength and aggression; rather, it is a game about balance and self-control. *You do not control your opponents in a poker game. You control yourself and adjust your play so that your opponents' excesses become their own undoing.*

* David Sklansky, *Theory of Poker,* 3rd Edition (Two Plus Two, Las Vegas, NV, 1994) pages 254-255.

GAME OBSERVATION FORM FOR ONLINE HOLD'EM

Cardroom/URL:	Game:
Date:	Stakes:
Start/End Time:	Participants:

HAND	RAISE PRE-FLOP	NUMBER PRE-FLOP	NUMBER POST-FLOP	SHOW DOWN	WINNING HAND	POT

NOTES:

Observing Online Games

Make photocopies of the form on the left and use them to assess online poker games. Observe the play of at least 10 hands. Assign sequential numbers to the hands in the first column. Make a check mark in the second column if there is a pre-flop raise. Note the number of players who pay to see the flop in the third column and the number of players who continue play after the flop in the fourth column. Make a check mark if there is a showdown and note the rank of the winning hand. Jot down the amount won in the last column.

Use the notes in considering the strategic questions posed on the previous page. Pay special attention to behavioral extremes, such as: always a showdown; never a showdown; everyone folds following a raise; everyone calls a raise. Approximate where the game falls on the strategic grid and plan your strategy before entering the game. It is especially important to observe online games carefully because social cues and player motivations are more difficult to discern in an online environment.

Part III

Putting it All Together

So far this book has provided a systematic outline of the principles for success at Texas Hold'em poker. What follows is a series of five essays on poker, and gambling, in general. The purpose of these essays is to discuss some counter-intuitive mathematical ideas and their relationship to human behavior that must be understood to succeed over the long run at any gambling endeavor.

The first three essays (Chapter 7) address probability theory. In my many years teaching math, I have found that probability concepts are among the most difficult for students to grasp. Part of the problem is our human tendency to believe that everything happens for a reason. It is difficult to accept the idea of events happening for no reason. People constantly search for patterns in sequences of random events, and, in fact, find patterns. However, patterns found within random event sequences have no predictive value. You will always be able to find patterns because humans are good at finding patterns— it is how we learn. But patterns found in a sequence of past random events will not predict the outcome of future random events, which is the essential meaning of randomness.

People also have a related tendency to project personal meaning into random events. When playing lotteries, horses and roulette, for example, we pick numbers that have personal meaning, such as our birthday, child's birthday, or anniversary. Because enough people pick meaningful numbers, over time the laws of chance dictate that some of these numbers will win on occasion. But again, accidental coincidence does not mean that these numbers are predictive in any way. It just means that people are good at finding meaning in the events that make up their lives. No one is willing to accept the fact that a good deal of the important events in our lives happen by chance.

Part of the difficulty with accepting the unpredictability of future random events, is that mathematically it is necessary to distinguish between two types of events—*independent* and *conditional*. Each time the deck is reshuffled and the cards dealt, all memory of the past is erased. Each starting hand is an independent event with its own unchanged probability. The first essay in Chapter 7 discusses probability concepts for independent events. Once a hand is dealt, probabilities become conditional. What is the probability of an Ace appearing on the board? If you hold two Aces, that probability is substantially reduced compared to the situation where you hold no Aces. If you hold two Aces and you have good reason to believe your opponents hold the other two, the probability of another Ace appearing has fallen to zero. The second essay in Chapter 7 discusses these kinds of situations where probabilities are altered because of conditions. Lastly, Chapter 7 discusses the mathematical requirements for winning over the long run. Randomness means that anything can happen in the short-run, but what happens if you play month after month, year after year?

Chapter 8 is a discussion of the psychological attributes necessary for success. Most poker books stress the need for patience. However, poker requires a different kind of patience than the kind your mother taught. Waiting for an event that can happen at any time is different from waiting for an event that will happen in a given amount of time. The first essay in Chapter 8 concerns the need for a new understanding of "patience." The last essay elaborates on the need for a flexible, dynamic strategy and how adjustments are made during a day of playing poker.

7. Mathematical Considerations

Past, Present and Future—
Do Probabilities Change?

I have a friend who believes that if you toss a coin three times, and it comes up heads each time, a greater than even chance exists for it to land tails on the fourth toss. If you question why she believes the probability changes, her answer is: "Over the long-run the coin must land heads as often as tails, so if a streak of heads occurs, a tail becomes more probable since even numbers of each must be maintained."

This fallacious belief that the coin's past history affects its future is fun to explore with further questions. Examples:

- Suppose I flip the coin three times and it comes up three heads, then I put it away. Tomorrow I take it out again. Is the probability still greater that a tail will occur? If the probability is greater, what happens if I wait a week or a month or a year?

- If after some elapsed time interval (day, week, month), the probabilities reset to 50-50, why does this happen?

- If there is no time interval that resets the probabilities to 50-50, how do I know it wasn't due for three heads in a row? After all, I may have just received the coin, so how do I know the previous owner hadn't flipped it five times and gotten all tails?

97

- How exactly has the probability changed of a tail occurring after three heads in a row? What will it be if just one head has appeared, or after five heads in row?

If my friend's belief is true, all these questions should have answers. The fact that all answers to these questions would be nonsense shows the belief is false.

Of course, a more profitable exercise would be to find a betting person who believes that a past sequence of coin flips affects the future. If this person is willing to pay better than even money on the outcome of a fourth head each time three heads appear in a row, you are assured of making money. Since past coin flips have no affect on future ones, the probabilities remain 50-50. Anyone willing to pay out better than even money on wagers against coin flips—even selected coin flips that occur after streaks—will lose over the long-run.

I relate the story of my friend's belief in coin flips because it is easy to see that the belief is wrong. However, many gamblers share the same wrong belief and don't realize it. They will behave as if the past does affect the future. Examples of common behaviors:

- You have just lost seven hands in a row at blackjack. You decide to bet the table maximum on the eighth hand because it must be time for a win. After all, how often do you lose eight hands in a row?

- You have received garbage poker hands for the last hour and decide that no matter what, you will bet heavily on the next hand because it must be time for a winning hand.

- You repeatedly play the same lottery numbers, believing that if those numbers haven't won yet, their time must be coming.

Each of these behaviors results from believing that "I'm due." Claiming that "I'm due" is just another way of claiming that the past affects the future.

There are more subtle expressions of this wrong thinking, such as believing that other players in the game affect the probabilities. Examples:

- Some poker players believe that the more players there are competing for a pot, the more likely it is that they will be dealt three-of-a-kind or better. It is easy to fall into this trap, since winning hands tend to be higher when there are more players at the table. Three of a kind is much more likely to be the winning hand when seven players compete, while with two players, a high pair is often enough to win. However, winning hands are higher, only because more hands are dealt, and to win, you have to beat more people. Whatever the number of players, the probability of you, an individual, receiving three-of-a-kind is always the same. Present events, such as the number of players who decide to fold early, do not after the fact affect the probabilities on the past event of the deal. Just as the past doesn't affect the future, the present does not affect the past.

- Some poker players believe in betting heavily during winning streaks and advise not to leave the table. This may be sound advice if the reasons for the winning streak have to do with being at a table filled with bad players. However, if the reason is a sudden streak of great cards, there is no reason to believe this has anything to do with the table, your seat, your opponents, the dealer, the day of the week, the color of your socks, or any factor, period. Good streaks happen just like bad streaks. There are no reasons; that is just the nature of a series of random events.

Make sure that your playing decisions are grounded in correct reasons. Analyze the reasons for your decisions. If the reason comes down to believing that the past affects the future, the reason is wrong.

Behaviors that Change the Odds

Many players understand that probabilities do not change from hand to hand. They know that an unseen card has an equal chance of being any one of the remaining unseen cards. However, they fall into the trap of treating all cards not in their hand as unseen cards. Cards held by your opponents are not unseen cards. Your opponents have seen them and their actions are a source of information. Only one card is out that beats you, but if your opponent acts like she has that one card, don't think that being beaten is unlikely. Many players make the mistake of playing only their cards and never asking the question: Why are my opponents still in the hand?

On a St. Louis riverboat a number of years ago, the following hand occurred at my table. After the deal, a player in an early position raised pre-flop. Except for one player who called the raise, everyone else folded. The player who initially raised—I will call Player 1— had played a tight game all afternoon. I had observed one other pre-flop raise from him earlier that day and it came on pocket Aces, so I took his raise as a sign of strength. He also appeared to be a regular (the casino employees all knew him by name and greeted him warmly). Players who are regulars at certain cardrooms often play tight, solid games. Otherwise, they can't afford to be regulars. The player who called his raise, Player 2, called without hesitation, so I also put him on a strong hand. The flop came up A, 10, 6. Player 1 bet; Player 2 called. The turn card was an Ace. Player 1 bet and again Player 2 called. The river card fell as a K. Player 1 bet and Player 2 raised. Player 1 countered with a re-raise. In this cardroom, the rule was that if two players went head-to-head on the end, raises were not capped. The rule allowed players to get into a raising war as long as they had money on the table. Player 2 re-raised and the war was on. At this point, it was obvious to me what each player held. Player 1 must have had pocket Aces and Player 2 pocket Kings. Four Aces beats Kings-full but Player 2 seemed oblivious to that possibility. He continued to counter each re-raise with another. Finally, Player 1 decided he had taken enough of Player 2's money, put down a final re-raise and exposed his two Aces. Player 2 showed his two Kings and shook his head in disbelief.

Losing with Kings-full to four Aces is a highly improbable bad beat. I'd raise, too, if I hit Kings-full at the river, but with this board, would I completely discount the possibility of my opponent having the remaining two Aces or even one Ace and the remaining King? Player 2 with Kings-full has seen 7 cards, which leaves 45 unseen cards, 2 of which his opponent has. Pick 2 cards from 45 unseen cards and there are 990 possibilities, only three of which (AK, AA, AK) beat Kings-full for this board. However, Player 1's cards are not two random unseen cards from 990 possible combinations. He has seen them and acted in such a way that eliminates from consideration almost all of these 990 possibilities. Player 1 would not be re-raising if he held 2, 5 or J, 7 or 4, 8, so why is he re-raising? It is not correct for Player 2 to assume that the odds of losing are remote (3 in 990), given Player 1's behavior.

Many beginners make the mistake of Player 2 above: They only play their cards and never consider why their opponents are in the hand. As a further example of how behaviors change the probabilities, consider a hand I played in the now-defunct Prince George's County Maryland cardrooms.

I was playing $5-$10 Omaha when a woman joined the game, sitting to my left, whose play immediately changed the dynamics of the table (See the Appendix I for an explanation of Omaha). She played very aggressive poker and rarely called. Her actions were bet, raise, or fold, and she played in most of the hands. She raised pre-flop, regardless of her position, for almost every hand. Since I sat on her right, I knew that any bet I called would be raised, so I tightened my starting requirements for hands, folding hands I ordinarily would call with, calling with my premium hands and letting her put in the raise for me. I was the only player at the table who made this adjustment. Everyone else, seeing that her pre-flop raises conveyed little information, called her raise. Soon almost every player at the table called her pre-flop raise every single hand. With so much money seeding the pot, no one wanted to fold before seeing the flop. The entry of this one player changed the entire table dynamics, causing an extremely loose-aggressive game to develop.

In a loose-aggressive game, so-called "bad beats" are actually highly probable. One hand in particular stands out as an example of how the new table dynamics distorted the probabilities. Of my four starting cards, two were Kings. I called, she put in her raise, and every single person at the table (there were eleven including me) called her raise. The three cards that came on the flop were K, A, and 8, all of different suits. I bet my set of Kings. She raised, the man to her immediate left called her raise, and everyone else dropped returning the action back to me. Because two players were up against me after seeing the flop, I thought it likely that each had an Ace and possibly one of them had an Ace, 8, giving them Aces-over. My three Kings had to be the top hand so I re-raised. She called, a first for her that day; he called. The turn card came, a 3 of the only suit not yet on the board (There would be no flush possible). I bet, she called, and he called. Her sudden respect for my bets and his refusal to go away convinced me they both had Aces-over.

The river card was an Ace. Had I been going against one player, I would have checked. But I knew I would not be raised since each of them had to fear the other. I bet my Kings-full (since I knew I had to call with it). If you know you are going to call, and do not fear a raise, take the initiative and bet. Your opponents might not have hit their draw and could fold. In this case, they had hit. Both of them called and each turned over an Ace, 8. As the dealer stacked the chips into two piles in order to split the pot between them, he shook his head in disbelief and said to me: "That was the *only* card that could beat you."

But how improbable was that last card being the one remaining Ace? My two opponents each have four cards and I "know" they each have an Ace. That means there is only one remaining Ace among the 36 cards that are not part of our three hands or the board. The odds appear to be 1 in 36 or 2.7%, the fact that shocked the dealer.

However, given the behavior of the players at the table, this assessment is not accurate. Think about the table dynamics. Every single person called this woman's pre-flop raise. When an Ace showed on the flop, no one holding an Ace would have dropped. Her raise pre-flop scared no one; neither would her raise after the flop have scared anyone holding an Ace. The man to her left didn't scare, and with 11 pre-flop raises ($110) in the pot, anyone with a chance to win would have stayed. When the other eight people at the table folded a total of 32 cards after the flop, *it meant none of those cards was an Ace.* When the dealer reached for the river card, only four cards remained in the deck and one of them had to be an Ace. The odds of me being beaten were 1 in 4. As the favorite, my bets and raises were correct, but my loss was not a great improbability.

In the previous section, I explained that the distribution of cards to players and the board are completely random events with no memory of the past. However, once the cards are dealt and players have seen them and acted, events cannot be considered random. The probability of a four falling on the board may be the same as an Ace, but an Ace is much more likely to have paired someone than a four. Many players keep any hand containing an Ace, but almost no one keeps every hand that contains a four. To be successful, you need to put your opponents on hands and play accordingly. Do not think only of your cards and the probability that a random unseen hand is better. Always ask yourself: "Why are my opponents acting the way they are?"

Requirements for Success

To gamble successfully, you must:

- Have a sufficient bankroll
- Place bets with positive expectations
- Accumulate statistics

Having a sufficient bankroll means that the size of a typical bet must be small in comparison to your total bankroll so that normally occurring losses do not wipe you out. In the movie, *Rounders*, the hero, an expert Hold'em player, violates this rule when he wagers his entire bankroll on a single hand of high-stakes, no limit Hold'em. He is dealt A♣ 9♣. The flop is A♠ 8♣ 9♠. Figuring his opponent is on a spade draw, he bets his two pair. He is thrilled with the turn card (9♥) giving him 9's full. When the river card is a 3♠, he figures his opponent has made his spade flush and will call any bet. He goes all in with his entire bankroll ($30,000). This is a good bet because his opponent cannot have two nines, is unlikely to have the other two Aces, and will be hesitant to fold a flush. The problem: the remaining two Aces is exactly what his opponent has. Aces-full beat nines-full and in the next scene our hero is back to his day job. Despite his poker expertise, he is unable to buy into any games. The hero's mistake wasn't how he played, it was wagering everything he had on one hand.

Placing bets with positive expectations means that if the bet is won, the payoff is greater than the odds against winning. In other words, the pot odds must be favorable. Over the long run, you cannot win money if you consistently place bets with unfavorable payoffs. Many poker players always draw to certain hands. If they need one card to complete a flush or a straight, they will stay in the hand no matter how much it costs or how much money is at stake. With one card to come, completing a flush or open-ended straight happens about one out of every five tries. If the payoff isn't at least 5 to 1, you are losing money because your one win every five tries will not be enough to pay for the inevitable four losses. Just because you will win a certain percentage of these bets, doesn't mean you should make them. Accumulating statistics means that many, many bets must be placed. It is this third condition that most people fail to understand. Most books on gambling state the need for a sufficient bankroll and teach how to place bets with positive expectations (good bets) and avoid bets with negative expectations (bad bets). While this knowledge is necessary, it is not sufficient to be a winner. What is often glossed over is the necessity of accumulating statistics.

The reason for this omission is that accumulating statistics is work. The attraction of gambling is the possibility of wealth without work. But the truth is, *successful gamblers must work hard for their winnings.*

To illustrate why all three conditions must be present, consider one form of gambling: selling life insurance.

You start a company selling life insurance, and you sell your first policy to a 20-year old person in good health for $100. You agree to pay $100,000 if that person should die within a year. Since the odds of a person that age dying within a year are about 10,000 to 1, it is very unlikely that you will have to pay out any money. But suppose a freak accident befalls that person tomorrow. If you do not have a sufficient bankroll, you will be bankrupt before you have a chance to sell another policy.

If you do have a sufficient bankroll, the bet you placed does have a positive expectation. You are offering to pay at a rate of 1000 to 1 for an event that has 10,000 to 1 odds against occurring. Suppose your customer refuses to pay $100 for the policy so you lower the price to $1. At this price, your customer will eagerly buy your policy, but you have just placed a bet with a negative expectation. You agreed to pay at a rate of 100,000 to 1 for an event that has 10,000 to 1 odds against occurring. However, there is a strong temptation on your part to sell the policy for $1, because the chances of the person dying have not changed. The odds are overwhelming that at the end of the year you will be $1 richer. Your sale is much easier and pocketing $1 is better than nothing.

The temptation to sell the policy for $1 illustrates a paradox associated with gambling. Whatever price the life insurance policy sells for, the odds are overwhelmingly in favor of you keeping the money. However $1 is a bad bet that should be avoided and $100 is a good bet that should be made.

The difference between good and bad bets only becomes apparent when statistics are accumulated—after you do the work of selling many life insurance policies. If you sell 10,000 policies, it becomes a certainty that at least one person will die. If you charged $1 each, the $10,000 collected does not cover one loss. Your business is headed for bankruptcy. However, if you sell 10,000 policies at $100 each, the million dollars collected covers 10 deaths. While it is almost certain that at least one customer will die, it is extremely unlikely that 10 will die. Your business has to make money.

Anything can happen to a single customer. Therefore, a good bet (the $100 policy) could lose and a bad bet (the $1 policy) could win. If you sell only one policy, knowledge of mortality rates is useless. Knowing the difference between good and bad bets pays off only when statistics are accumulated, *and it is only through the accumulation of statistics that you are assured of making money.*

The strategies for playing poker described in this book are designed to maximize your expectations for winning over the long run, *as you accumulate statistics.* However, even when bets are correctly made and hands correctly played, the outcome of any given hand or any given playing session is uncertain.

Poker is a deceptive game because good players don't always win and bad players don't always lose. There are statistical fluctuations in the outcomes. Your goal should be to make the right decisions for the right reasons. You should not get upset or elated over outcomes of single hands. Only as time passes and trends become clear, is it possible to evaluate the quality of your decision-making.

8. Psychological Considerations

Choose Your Battles

How often have you entered into a dispute that afterwards you judged as not worth it? It could be a price dispute at a store, an annoying action of a co-worker, or a trivial argument with a family member. In the end, winning or losing didn't matter. The most you could have hoped to gain would never compensate for the cost in time, effort, or ill-will generated. With experience, you learn to avoid confrontations that in the long run are not worth the cost. We all have our "principles," but savvy people choose their battles. They know when it is worth taking a stand and when it better to let things go.

In poker, learning to choose the right battles is crucial to success and it is perhaps the hardest skill to learn. Your first impulse in any confrontation is to act. You come to the poker table to compete for the pot. Watching others vie for the money feels counter to that goal. How is folding hand after hand competing? Inaction also leads to complacency. You stop paying close attention and then miss out on the opportunities that do occur. Poker is a fast-moving game and decisions must be made quickly. For these two reasons—the desire to compete and the need to stay alert—it is difficult to suppress the urge to play in most of the hands. Even if intellectually you know to fold, your emotions constantly urge you to make exceptions.

All books on poker correctly state that the number one mistake most beginners make is *to play in too many hands*. Be patient and wait for the right situation and cards is the standard advice. This advice is sound, but in my opinion, it is poorly expressed because patience is the wrong idea. Patience is what you need waiting in line at the bank, waiting for the light to turn green, waiting for an unproductive meeting to end. In all these cases, you know when your goal—banking, driving, returning to useful work—will be reached. Patience is accepting that your goal will come in its own time, that it cannot be rushed. Also, being patient means that if you pass the time daydreaming, nothing is lost.

Contrast waiting in line with waiting for a decent hand in a poker game. In poker, you never know when your goal—a favorable betting opportunity—will occur. You must be mentally alert and ready for action at all times because at any time, you might have to act. In the meantime, unfavorable betting opportunities are constantly present, tempting you to take foolish chances. Rather than patience, what you need to learn is what I call "deliberate non-action." *You must understand that not acting is one of the most important actions in poker.* You must accept the counter-intuitive idea that not taking action is an integral part of the game and essential to your long-range goal of making money.

If folding is not your most frequent action, you are playing badly. It is nice to wish for hand after hand of great cards, such as pocket Aces and pocket Kings occurring several times per hour. You fantasize about betting forcefully as both of your pocket cards pair up on the flop, while your opponents shrink back in fear. There will be times when these events happen, times when you can do no wrong and winning is easy. There also will be long hours, even long days, of hand after hand of garbage. During these times, your chip pile gets eaten away by the blinds, the few good starting hands you get don't hit on the flop, and the game seems utterly pointless and futile.

Poker encompasses both euphoria and frustration. It is impossible to have one without the other because over the long-run, statistics rule. Play in enough hands and the distribution of cards received and draws hit approaches the percentages in the charts. The problem with poker is that you have no control over the good times and bad times. The nature of randomness means that events happen with no discernable pattern. You are never due for either a good streak or a bad streak. Whatever your thoughts are—however alert you feel, however ready you are for action—your mental state will not change the distribution of the cards.

While alertness does not change the cards, it does affect the one thing you do control: the decisions you make. Again, this is why patience is the wrong idea. Being patient means you fall into a routine of automatic decisions that dulls your thinking and causes you to loose your edge. Alertness is required at all times and to stay alert, you must think of non-action as a deliberate action.

Consider the outcome of a hand at my table one afternoon in an Atlantic City casino. A showdown occurred between two players with a board of mediocre cards: 6♣, 2♠, 5♥, 6♦, 9♥. Expecting boring hands, none of us at the table, including the dealer, paid close attention. One of the players showed 2♦, 5♦, and having matched both his pocket cards, claimed the pot. The other player with a 5♣, 10♣ didn't object so the dealer pushed the chips to the player with 5's over 2's and set up for another hand. Only after the transaction ended, did a few of us at the table wake up and realize that the pot had been awarded to the losing hand. By then, it was too late to change the outcome.

When you first read this, did you immediately see that the 5, 10 is the winning hand? The 2's are completely irrelevant because the board has a pair of 6's. That means each player's hand consists of the same two pairs—5's and 6's. The kicker (fifth card) decides the hand and since the 10♣ is higher than all other cards on the board, it beats the 9♥ on the board. (If a card higher than a 10 was on the board, say a Jack, the players would share the same kicker and the pot is split. The best five-card hand for each player in that case would be 5's and 6's with a Jack kicker, and the 10 does not play.) By not analyzing the situation, the player with the winning hand lost an entire pot, potentially the difference between a profitable and an unprofitable playing session.

Deliberate non-action means you don't let the routine take the edge off your play. To stay focused, analyze the actions of the players and dealers, and take breaks. Be mentally alert at all times and ready to act. Over time, small mistakes add up to big losses and small victories add up to big profits. If you are not paying attention at a crucial time, as in the example above, you lose money. But if staying focused requires you to contest every pot, you also lose money.

The concept of tight-aggressive play is to forcefully contest pots only when you have the edge. Keep mentally focused by careful observation of the other players when the odds are against you. Choose only battles where you are the favorite, and don't feel that you have to win every time. If you select the best situations to challenge your opponents and ignore the marginal ones, you will accumulate money over time.

Alan Schoonmaker explains in his book *The Psychology of Poker,** that the successful tight-aggressive style for poker is unnatural. In his observation, only in the professions of fighter pilot and police officer are there people capable of tightly controlled aggression. Tight people are naturally cautious while aggressive people tend to take chances. The combination of the two traits results only from a deliberate training process. It does not happen on its own.

* Alan Schoonmaker, *The Psychology of Poker*, (Two Plus Two, Las Vegas, NV, 2000) page 248.

Adjust Your Play to Conditions

A common technique for training people to make critical decisions in real-time, under stress, is the use of computer simulations as a substitute for experience. Need to learn how to land a fully loaded 747 airliner in a thunderstorm with half of its engines out? With modern computer simulators, a pilot can practice this maneuver repeatedly without risking lives. Police trainees learn how to use their weapons by practicing with life-size videos of realistic encounters. They learn when it is correct to shoot someone and when it is a mistake, again without actual lives being at risk.

For game players, computers are programmed to simulate opponents. Without actual money or prestige on the line, students of a game can spend hours practicing under realistic conditions. Chess players, for example, routinely train with personal computers against inexpensive computer programs that play at the master level. While computers play chess differently than humans, that difference has become harder to detect. For the average chess player, it is difficult to beat a computer. Today, chess programs that run on powerful machines routinely beat grandmasters. If you want a strong opponent, with infinite patience, to teach you chess, computers are a good substitute. Learn to play chess well against a computer and you are on your way to beating people.

Can you learn poker by playing against a computer? There are computer simulations of live casino poker available for purchase. I recommend use of poker programs to teach the mechanics of the game, how to act in turn, place bets, read cards, and count winnings. But be warned, success against a computer tells you nothing about success against people. Unlike in chess, it is easy for a mediocre poker player to beat a computer. It is also instructive to examine the reasons why the two games (chess and poker) are so different in this respect.

Chess has a clearly defined object: checkmate your opponent's King. All chess moves and the plans motivating them have checkmate as their long-range goal. Since checkmate is easily defined mathematically, programming the computer's goal is straightforward.

Poker also has a straightforward object: to win money. The problem is that money means different things to different people, and to a computer, money means nothing. To complicate matters further, money can mean different things to the same person. When I play poker on the first Friday of every month, year after year, with the same six friends, the motivation is to socialize and be entertained. The difference between a good or bad night is whether I win or lose $20. That is not a meaningful amount of money to any of us. The result is an evening where we play loose junk poker games that require no strategic thinking.

When I play in Atlantic City, I behave differently. I risk several hundred dollars with the goal of winning a few hundred. To me, that amount of money is meaningful, but not an amount so large that it will cause me financial harm if I lose. Unlike Friday night poker, the games I play in are tightly structured. My motivation is the thrill of competition. I put on a game face and think carefully about the decisions I make. I feel good when I win, frustrated when I lose.

I do not play Hold'em at the $10–20 level or above. At these stakes, I would have to risk one or more thousand dollars. I can afford to lose a thousand dollars, but I am unwilling to. There would be no fun playing with money that I would be unwilling to lose. I would be unable to make correct decisions. Constantly, I would think about the money, rather than whether the bet or raise I was making was right for the situation.

I certainly would not risk an amount of money that could lead to financial ruin. If you routinely risk financial ruin in any activity (poker, blackjack, slots, investing, shopping), you have a serious problem and should immediately stop the activity and seek professional help. For poker to be a meaningful competitive activity, the amount of money at stake has to be large enough that players find it worth winning and protecting, but not so large that they fear losing.

I have told you my motivations and budget limitations. Each of my opponents has a different set of reasons for playing and a different budget. Even though we play in the same game, the meaning of the money is different for each of us. At a poker table, why people play the way they do depends not so much on the cards they are dealt, but what the money means to them and their reasons for playing. That means I must adjust my play to them.

It is the inability to adjust that makes computer programs bad for poker. Chess players must adjust to changing situations, but not in the same way poker players do. Chess positions usually have a best plan of action and often a best move. It is the position that matters, not the opponent. Chess players are taught to always assume their opponent will make the best move and plan accordingly. If their opponent fails to make the best move, the task usually becomes easier. Mastering chess involves learning thousands of positions and the best plan of action for each of them. However, in poker, best play depends not on the cards, but the situation. Players must make continual adjustments to their underlying strategy. For the same cards, correct strategy may change completely depending on the situation. Consider a five-hour session I had playing poker in Atlantic City.

1st hour (late morning): I began at a full table and everyone played in almost every hand. Passive play ruled—no one raised pre-flop or in any other betting rounds. Mostly players called. In this environment, I played looser than otherwise. Drawing hands became profitable because I could see the flop cheaply and know that a big pot waited for me if I hit the draw. Drawing hands were playable from almost any position since I "knew" everyone would call and no one would raise. I had to fold high pairs quickly if they didn't improve on the flop, because with so many people in the hand, someone always hit a draw. It generally took trips or better to win, and with the pots large, there was always a showdown, so there was no point in trying to bluff. The big pots also covered my mistakes.

2nd hour (lunch time): The game was frequently short-handed because players kept leaving for 20–30 minute intervals to eat. Sometimes only 5 to 6 players were present which lead to confusion on blinds, since people kept missing their blind. My cost to play went up because I stayed at the table, so my blind position came up more frequently. Players remained passive. I played aggressively, especially with big pairs and premium starting cards. Drawing hands became unplayable from any position since there were so few players to contribute to the pot. Two pair, especially if one was large, often won. Fewer showdowns occurred, so I stole some pots with aggressive raising. I needed to steal pots or the frequent blinds would eat up my chip pile.

3rd hour (early afternoon): The table filled with aggressive players. Almost always a pre-flop raise occurred. Playing cards appropriate for my position became critical. I could not limp in with weak starting cards because I would be raised. I needed to have premium starting cards and be prepared to raise or call a raise to stay in a hand. Mistakes became costly since the aggressive play meant I paid dearly to chase.

4th hour (mid-afternoon): The action dried up and the game tightened considerably. Most players folded their starting cards. Whether my hand was mediocre or a monster didn't matter much since I couldn't attract bettors either way. With little money in play, my earnings potential dropped to near nothing. While keeping my seat, I started scouting other tables, considering a switch.

5th hour (late afternoon): Frustration with the lack of action set in. Someone raised pre-flop, there was a re-raise, and then someone yelled "cap it." Everyone put in three bets to see a flop. Suddenly, the entire table was on a tilt. Chips flew everywhere, even when players held the flimsiest of cards. Wild swings occurred in everyone's bankroll. To play profitably, I needed a lot of money and the very best cards. Playing with anything less than premium cards from any position wasn't worth it, because the pre-flop expenses became too high. I needed to be a heavy favorite pre-flop to justify putting up so much money.

Notice that as the day progressed, strategy that was correct one hour became incorrect later on. This is hardly ever true at chess, where a strong move is always a strong move. Poker players must constantly adjust to the changing social dynamic. Computers are very poor at adjusting.

The great British mathematician, Alan Turing, argued in a famous article entitled "Computer Machinery and Intelligence" published in 1950 in the philosophical journal, *Mind*, that a computer could be said to "think" if interacting with the computer proved indistinguishable from interacting with a human. Put a human and the computer in two separate rooms, and allow a human to interrogate them unseen. If the interrogator, through a series of probing questions, can't distinguish the computer's answers from the human's, the computer is said to pass the "Turing Test" and, according to Turing, is actually thinking.

Restrict interactions to the microcosm of chess, and computers today can almost pass the Turing Test. Based on chess moves alone, it is difficult for the expert to distinguish a human grandmaster from a computer. But when it comes to poker, is the Turing Test even meaningful? There is an insidious problem with programming computers to play poker that in my opinion raises the Turing test to a higher level. The problem is not whether people can figure out if they are up against a computer. It is whether the computer can figure out people, especially the ever changing social dynamics in a randomly selected group of people. Nobody at a poker table would care whether or not the computer played poker like a person. In fact, people would welcome a computer, since computers tend to play predictably. Computers are, by definition, predictable, which is the meaning of the word "programmed." If you play a computer simulation for a short amount of time, you will learn the machine's betting patterns, adjust your play, and soon win consistently. But predictability doesn't mean the computer is distinguishable from a person. Many people play poker as predictably as a computer. They are welcomed at the table, too. If you find a predictable poker opponent and learn his or her patterns, you can exploit that knowledge for profit.

Most people, however, are unpredictable and human unpredictability is an advantage at poker. To play poker successfully, computers not only have to develop human unpredictability, they must learn to adjust to human unpredictability as well. Computers fail miserably at the problem of adjusting to ever-changing social conditions that result from human interactions. That is why beating a computer at poker is so easy. Of course, the same requirement, the ability to adjust to unpredictability, applies to poker-playing humans who want to be successful. Go back and study how I adjusted each hour in my poker session. However, as humans, we are more accustomed to human unpredictability, so we are far better at learning how to adjust.

Part IV

Where to Go from Here

This book is intended to be both a beginning and a guide. After reading to this point, you should be able to hold your own in the typical low-limit Hold'em games found in public cardrooms and casinos. However, since Hold'em is a rich, complex, and changing game, there is much more to learn. A number of valuable books exist on Hold'em and poker, in general. The strategic framework outlined in Chapter 6 is meant to guide both your approaches to playing poker and your comprehension of further readings on poker. This last section of the book contains information on further reading and places to play.

In preparing this book, I read extensively on poker and Hold'em. In Chapter 9, I summarize books on Hold'em and books on poker, in general, that influenced me the most. The Web also contains a wealth of information, much of it free to Web-surfers. I summarize the contents of some of the major Web sites devoted to poker. Most of these Web sites have updated links to further information.

Of course the real fun in poker isn't reading, it is playing. Chapter 10 has information on places to play, both in person and online. The list is not comprehensive and is only as up-to-date as the publication of this book, but it shows that playing opportunities exist in many locations throughout the country.

9. Resources

Books on Texas Hold'em

The Complete Book of Hold 'Em Poker, by Gary Carson, Kensington Publishing, http://www.kensingtonbooks.com, (2001). A comprehensive book on Hold'em that covers basic and advanced concepts. Carson makes an insightful argument that your theoretical perspective on poker must be matched to the game conditions. He articulates a total of eight theoretical views of poker. Two examples: "Poker is a game of money and odds." "Poker is a contest between a made hand and a drawing hand." He argues that to be successful, your theoretical view of poker must be matched to the game conditions.

This book also contains one of the best discussions of starting hand values that I have read. The author goes beyond the usual rankings of starting hands and explains the impact of position on the their value. In Carson's theory, the value of a starting hand depends on the game conditions and he provides an in-depth explanation of how the nature of the game (tight, loose, aggressive, passive) affects the play of specific starting hands. Aside from his theories, Carson has worthwhile insights on a number of poker aspects, such as table image, player stereotypes, women and poker, cheating, and at the end of the book, an extremely clear explanation of the mathematics for calculating poker probabilities.

Hold'em Excellence From Beginner to Winner, 2nd Edition, by Lou Krieger, ConJelCo, http://www.conjelco.com, (2000). Lou Krieger writes lucid and entertaining prose that is fun to read. I think it is no accident that he is also a co-author of the *Poker for Dummies®* book discussed separately in the next section on books on poker. The meat of *Hold'em Excellence* is Part II, which is an extensive discussion of typical decisions that must be made in a hand at each stage. He discusses the different types of starting hands (suited connectors, large, medium, and small pairs) and how the play of each is affected by position. Included is a presentation of the differing opinions on the play of Ace-King. Part III of the book covers a variety of advanced topics, including computers in poker, strategic adjustments for jackpot games, and playing poker for a living. If you fantasize about playing poker professionally, this part of the book will snap you back to reality. Even if you are an excellent poker player, a pure mathematical analysis shows that poker is a tough way to earn a living. Your current day job is probably much more lucrative.

Hold 'em Poker, by David Sklansky, Two Plus Two Publishing, http://www.twoplustwo.com, (1997). This book was originally published in 1976 and has gone through several editions. It is the first book on Hold'em written by a professional player, and its strategies are geared more towards professional-level, tight-aggressive games. A feature of this book is Sklansky's ranking of starting hands. Of the 169 possible starting hands, he identifies 72 to be given consideration for play. The 72 starting hands are classified into eight groups that are ranked with Group 1 hands being the strongest through Group 8 as the weakest. The "Sklansky Hand Groups" are referred to frequently in discussions and writings on Hold'em, so it is useful to become familiar with the terminology and his reasoning for ranking the hands the way he did. Sklansky's discussion of desirable flops is applicable to tight games and counter-intuitive to those moving up from low-limit loose games to high-limit tight games. Overall *Hold'em Poker* has become a very influential book in the poker world.

Hold 'em Poker for Advanced Players, 3rd Edition, by David Sklansky and Mason Malmuth, Two Plus Two Publishing, http://www.twoplustwo.com, (1999). This is one of the most successful poker books ever written. All Hold'em players should give this book a careful read and think through the reasoning behind all the examples. Earlier editions of this book were geared toward strategies for professional-level tight aggressive games. However, the third edition has a significantly more material and includes discussions of other kinds of games. The analyses of "wild" games (extremely loose-aggressive) and short-handed games (1–3 opponents) are valuable.

It is not uncommon for Hold'em players to find themselves at short-handed games, especially during mealtimes or when tables are started. Short-handed games can be fun because more hands are playable, but strategy adjustments are required. Rather than avoid short-handed games, as many players do, it is worth acquiring the skills to profit from them.

More Hold'em Excellence: A Winner for Life, by Lou Krieger, ConJelCo, http://www.conjelco.com, (1999). This book goes beyond the first one on Hold'em Excellence, which was aimed primarily at beginners, to tackle more advanced concepts. Included are discussions of game selection, seat selection, tells, and how to take advantage of the most common mistakes made by low-limit Hold'em players. Strategies for loose-aggressive games are discussed at length.

Both of Krieger's Hold'em Excellence books have a color-coded "Start Chart" to assist players in deciding whether or not to play their first two starting cards. The chart weighs the factors of card strength and position, for determining whether a hand should be played or folded. The four-color format assists in reading and memorization. The chart is good resource for online players who can view charts while they play.

Winner's Guide to Texas Hold'em Poker, by Ken Warren, Cardoza Publishing, http://www.cardozapub.com, (1996). Warren's book is directed at low-limit Hold'em games which he defines as "games populated primarily by unskilled players." These games are loose-passive in nature with most hands ending in a showdown. His book is filled with practical advice. Since you need the cards to win at showdown, Warren advocates patient, straight-up play that will let profits accrue from your opponents' mistakes. The end of this book has extensive charts on hands and probabilities that are a useful reference.

Winning Low-Limit Hold'em, 2nd Edition, by Lee Jones, ConJelCo, http://www.conjelco.com, (2000). The strategy in this book is targeted towards the typical $3–6 Hold'em game, which is one of the most popular in cardrooms and online. By "low-limit," Jones means loose games (passive and aggressive) where a large number of players pay to see the flop and often stick around after the flop with weak, nearly hopeless hands. This is a very readable book filled with solid advice on how to play your hands. Jones also explains which strategies are specific to loose games and why certain strategies appropriate for a loose game would fail in a tight game. Worthwhile discussions in this book include the concept of "dominated" hands and strategy in spread-limit games. A dominated hand is one like K, 4, unsuited, which if it hits the flop, will either always lose to a better hand or not get any action. Dominated hands are kinds of trash hands that are tempting to play in loose games, but should be avoided. Spread-limit games (a variation described in Chapter 2) require a slightly different strategic thinking because of the possibility of seeing flops more cheaply than in a structured game. The quiz format at the end of each chapter provides an interactive way of testing your ability to incorporate the advice into decisions.

General Books on Poker

Poker for Dummies®, by Richard D. Harroch and Lou Krieger, IDG Books Worldwide Inc., http://www.dummies.com (2000). Consistent with all the Dummies® books, this provides a light and breezy overview of the world of poker, complete with numerous sub-headings, boxes, tips, summaries and cartoons. Basic strategies are summarized for the common cardroom games: Seven-Card Stud, and Texas Hold'em; and the High-Low split games, Seven-Card Stud Eight or Better, and Omaha Eight or Better. This book also serves as an excellent reference if you are setting up a dealer's choice home game and need the definitions of variants, such as Baseball, Razz, Black Mariah, Indian Poker and Crisscross. Also provided is a good overview of tournament poker, Internet poker, and video poker.

The Psychology of Poker, by Alan N. Schoonmaker, Ph.D., Two Plus Two Publishing, http://www.twoplustwo.com, (2000). Schoonmaker, a psychologist, writes with frankness and sincerity on how an individual's personality affects the way he or she plays poker. The purpose of the book is to "show you how you beat yourself and tell you how to stop doing it." The book invites you to rate your playing characteristics and those of your opponents, using a "styles" grid similar to the strategies grid I used in Chapter 6. Reading the book is an interactive experience with charts to fill out and quizzes to take, all designed to induce reflection on your own underlying motivations for playing poker. The four extreme playing styles, tight-passive, loose-passive, tight-aggressive and loose-aggressive, are characterized and discussed in detail with emphasis on the strengths, weaknesses, and adjustments needed for each playing style. By identifying how you play, you better understand how to overcome your weaknesses and exploit your strengths. In writing about himself, Schoonmaker explains that he prefers low-limit games because of the wider variety of playing styles found among the people who play these games. At the higher limits, the players become more serious and more alike in their approach to the game. To Schoonmaker, the profits are less important than having fun and learning about people. Overall, an insightful book that applies to all forms of poker.

Serious Poker, 2nd Edition, by Dan Kimberg, ConJelCo, http://www.conjelco.com, (2002). Kimberg, who maintains a large informational website on poker (see online resourses) provides an ambitious and comprehensive book that covers a tremendous amount of ground. Much of the material in his book is thought-provoking and unique, which you won't find elsewhere. The poker variants emphasized are the two most popular in cardrooms, Seven-Card Stud and Texas Hold'em. He describes the book as "an operator's manual for cardrooms," and the current 2nd edition of the book has a section on Internet play. A major strength of this book is that Kimberg teaches us how to think about poker, both at the table and away from it. As he explains, because poker is a fast-paced game, 99% of the thinking needs to be done away from the table. Among the topics included in this book are discussions of the luck versus skill factor, poker tournaments, detecting cheating methods, avoiding tells, and conducting home games. There is also a section at the end for the technically minded, with detailed mathematical explanations on probability concepts and their application to poker.

The Theory of Poker, by David Sklansky, Two Plus Two Publishing, http://www.twoplustwo.com, (1994). This is one of the most influential books on the subject of poker ever written. Sklansky discusses general concepts that apply to all variations of poker and includes examples from play in Hold'em, Seven-Card Stud, Five-Card Draw, and Lowball. The book presents the point of view of a professional poker player and the emphasis is on placing good bets, those that have a positive mathematical expectation. This is not an easy read because the mathematical analysis that accompanies his examples is at times complex. Often, for the purposes of computation, he assigns mathematical expectations to individual behaviors. For example, a play against an opponent who bluffs 30% of the time requires different strategy than an opponent who bluffs 5% of the time because the mathematical expectations are different when you bet. Assigning numbers to behaviors is a good technique for demonstrating why the strategies must be different. In practice, few players think about that at the table. Instead, they learn to judge the difference between opponents who bluff frequently, infrequently, or never.

Each chapter in the book is devoted to a particular poker concept. Examples include: slow playing, position, bluffing, semi-bluffing, pot odds, raising, and check-raising. Each concept is discussed in detail with multiple examples from different poker variations used to illustrate his thinking. A recurring theme is that good players must learn to adjust their play to conditions. Not only must the kind of game be considered (loose or tight), but the structure of the game as well. By structure, he means the limits in the betting rounds and the size of the antes in relation to the final pot. Limit Texas Hold'em is only one form of poker. If you consider participation in other poker variations, read Sklansky's discussion on game evaluation to determine what adjustments need to be made.

Zen and the Art of Poker, by Larry W. Phillips, Penguin Putnam Inc., http://www.penguinputnam.com, (1999). This is a book on mastering yourself and developing the state of mind necessary for success. Like Schoonmaker's book, the emphasis is on developing objectivity by separating ego and emotions from play. However, instead of the point-of-view of Western psychology, Phillips examines the Eastern "psychology" of Zen.

The book consists of a collection of 100 rules organized into five broad categories: (1) fundamentals, (2) establishing calmness and rhythm, (3) the "nuts and bolts" of play, (4) the "warrior" aspect of poker, and (5) understanding emotions and opponents. Most of the rules are related to mental preparedness, such as acquiring patience, reading opponents, accepting losses, and not going on a tilt. The advice applies to all forms of poker and specific tactical examples are not discussed.

Phillip's book on Zen and poker is a good complement to Schoonmaker's on psychology and poker. Both books have as a central theme that we defeat ourselves by being unaware of our own mental state. Each person's mental state brings limitations and flaws to poker play that you must be aware of, especially your own. However, the contrast in the approach these books take is fascinating. Western psychology analyzes, dissects, and charts behavior patterns with the goal of predicting future actions. All are necessary activities for understanding the reasons for and consequences of behaviors. Zen is about synthesis; it is about attaining a mental state where the complex behaviors needed to play winning poker come naturally.

The Zen point of view is interesting because I believe that the enjoyment of activities such as poker, or chess, or golf, comes from the suspension of time that occurs when we become totally immersed and no longer analyze our actions. Learning to perform an activity well means doing more while thinking less. As children, we worked hard to read and exerted considerable effort to understand spelling and sentence structure. As adults, we read without thinking about the act of reading. We only think about the mental world that our reading brings us into.

Online Resources

The Internet has many quality poker-related Web sites and much of the content is free. Here are locations and descriptions of selected sites that are particularly useful and rich in content.

General Information

http://www.intelligentpoker.com—is the companion Web site for this book. Changes that occur after this book is published will be posted on the Web site. Availability and offerings for online cardrooms is especially time sensitive and will be updated. Included are links to join online cardrooms, links to purchase books, and links to the home pages of most of the public cardrooms listed in Chapter 10.

http://www.pokerpages.com —is one of the top-ranked poker portals on the Web. It has comprehensive and up-to-date information for poker worldwide. The site offers: a database of poker establishments, daily-updated events and results, tips, seminars, and player profiles. Listen to live-audio broadcasts. Practice in free play-money tournaments. Communicate globally via forum and chat rooms. There is even a section for women in poker.

http://www.pokerschoolonline.com—is an online school for poker (presented by PokerPages described above). For $14.95 per month membership, you receive instruction—beginner through advanced levels—from poker professionals. Also, compete in play-money Multi-Table Tournaments, Satellites, and Ring Games, where over $100,000 worth of sponsorship points are available. Players who accumulate enough sponsorship points at the play-money games are awarded seats in real-money tournaments. The Poker School games are among the closest to the real world with the safety of play-money. This is a great way to learn tournament play without having to open a real-money account.

http://www.poker1.com—is the site for Mike Caro Unversity of Poker, a school for poker that is affiliated with Hollywood Park Casino (see Southern California Cardrooms on Page 147). Mike Caro, the legendary "Mad Genius" of poker, has many of his articles, columns, and lectures posted at this Web site. Also affiliated with Caro's site is United Poker Forum, which is an online message board for discussing any question, opinion, or issue related to poker.

Sources for Articles and News on Poker

Commitment to poker excellence requires continued reading and analysis of what others write. Here are some sites that have free articles on poker:

http://www.cardplayer.com—has many online articles by the most influential writers on poker. The site is also a great source for poker news and current events, including extensive coverage of tournaments throughout the United States.

http://www.playwinningpoker.com—poker professional Steve Badger maintains a large site with dozens of articles on strategy and online poker. His many subjects include Omaha strategy (see Appendix I for an explanation of Omaha), and the differences between online poker and in-person cardrooms. Selected articles are posted in multiple languages (Spanish, French, German, etc.).

http://www.poker.net—is an attractive site with articles, news, discussion forums, and links. They have a comprehensive directory of online cardrooms with ratings and profiles of each.

http://www.pokersearch.com—has online articles and a discussion forum. The site lists the locations and contact information for hundreds of cardrooms throughout the United States and assists in travel planning, including air and hotel reservations.

http://www.seriouspoker.com—is the companion web site for Dan
Kimberg's book, *Serious Poker*. Go here to learn more about his book
and read his articles written for *Card Player* magazine. He maintains
an extensive site with many useful links. Included are links for: book
reviews, tournament information, shopping for poker-related products, news, discussion groups, and articles by well known writers.

Publishers

Many of the publishers of books on poker maintain informative,
interactive, and entertaining Web sites. Some of the major sites are:

http://www.cardozapub.com—publishes over 100 titles on poker,
gaming, bridge, backgammon, and chess. There are books appropriate for every level of play, from novice to advanced.

http://www.conjelco.com—publishes books, newsletters, software,
and videos on poker and gambling-related products. Conjelco operates a large online store that sells products from other publishers at
discounted prices. Check out their "Gamblers Corner" for free information and links.

http://www.twoplustwo.com—publishes many of the most widely
known and influential books on poker and on gambling in general.
Their web site provides information on book titles and original essays by many of the authors. An online forum on poker topics is
operated through their web site. Anyone with a valid e-mail address
can register and participate in the discussions.

Statistical Information

https://www.pokerroom.com/evstats—Note the "s" after the http. You can also access this site via http://www.pokerroom.com and click on statistics. This is an interactive page that allows you to explore how some of the decision factors affect actual game results. The statistics presented are updated regularly because they are based on real-money Internet play and not a computer simulation. Use the pull-down menus to select a starting hand, a position to play from, the number of players competing, and the monetary stakes. Click on view statistics and the expected dollar amount won (expressed in number of big bets) is displayed. An instructive site for learning the strength of various starting cards and how that strength varies with position and number of players. As of this writing only 44 of the 169 possible starting hands produce positive results for the players. All others have negative expectation, meaning players lose money. Some notable hands with negative expectations are 22, 33, 44, and any hand containing an Ace with an unsuited card below a 10. In other words, those hands have tended to lose money.

10. Places to Play

Online Cardrooms

The following information is current as of February, 2003. Be advised that the Internet is in constant change. Links to Web sites and game availability can and do change overnight. Check the companion Web site for this book—http://ww.intelligentpoker.com—for updated information and for the most current access to online cardrooms. Online poker is a fast growing industry with many new cardrooms appearing during the past two years. The list that follows is a sampling of some of the major venues and their features. It is not meant to be comprehensive.

One additional note for Mac users: while most online cardrooms require the user to download software that runs on a Windows platform, it is possible to simulate Windows on a Macintosh. A software package called Virtual PC® made by Connectix at http://www.connectix.com, will simulate the Windows operating system on a Macintosh and allow the user to run Windows-based programs. Many of the software downloads from online cardrooms are known to run on a Macintosh that uses a Windows simulation. However, some trial and error might be required and only a few online cardrooms officially support the use of Windows simulation software.

For Windows users, exact system requirements vary with the cardroom. As a general rule, plan on having at least a Pentium processor and Windows 95 or later installed. The more elaborate poker interfaces require higher end computers. Before opening real-money acounts, experiment with several interfaces in play-money games, to find the ones that are most comfortable for both you and your computer.

America's Card Room has a program to pay *proposition* players willing to commit to 20 hours of play per week. (Proposition players are paid by the house to keep games going or get games started, but they play with their own money.)

> *URL:*http://www.americascardroom.com
> *Games Offered:* Fixed-limit Texas Hold'em, Seven-Card Stud, Seven-Card Stud High/Low Eight or Better, Omaha, Omaha High/Low Eight or Better.
> *Betting Limits:* Range from $0.50/$1 up to $20/$40.
> *Promotions:* Check their News area for current promotions.
> *Tournaments:* Check their tournament page.
> *Mac Compatible:* No
> *System Requirements:* Windows 98 or later (does not work with Windows 95) and a Pentium processor. Software download required.

DynamitePoker is an inexpensive way to start online poker. They offer Hold'em with nickel and dime betting limits and a variety of daily multi-table tournaments, some with buy-ins as lows as $1.50. Many of their tournaments feature bounty prizes on specific players as well as re-buys. As of this writing, only Hold'em and variations of Omaha are available, but Seven-Card Stud is planned for the future.

> *URL:* http://www.dynamitepoker.com
> *Games Offered:* Fixed-limit Texas Hold'em, Omaha, Omaha High/Low Eight or Better.
> *Betting Limits:* Range from $0.05/$0.10 up to $10/20.
> *Promotions:* Check their Promotions page for current offerings. Past promotions have included "freeroll" tournaments that have cash prizes but no entry fees.
> *Tournaments:* A wide variety offered, including private customized tournaments for groups of players on request.

Mac Compatible: Yes, but Macintosh use is not officially supported. Certain hardware/software combinations do work. Contact Dynamite Poker for advice.
System Requirements: Windows 95 or later. No software download required. Dynamite Poker works through a web browser using Java scripts. Must have a Java enabled web browser—Internet Explorer 4.01 or later/Netscape 4.x or later.

Guts Poker specializes in the "Guts" family of poker games. See the site for an explanation of Guts poker and its variants. Texas Hold'em is also offered, along with Stud games, and there are future plans for Omaha.

URL: http://www.gutspoker.com
Games Offered: Fixed-limit Texas Hold'em, Guts, Monte Carlo Guts, Three to Five Guts, Seven-Card Stud, Five-Card Stud.
Betting Limits: Range from $0.50/$1 up to $20/40
Promotions: Check their Promotions page for current offerings. Promotions have included sign-up bonuses, and daily high hand and weekly bad beat bonuses.
Tournaments: At the time of this writing tournaments were not available. Their tournament software is under development and should be ready in the future.
Mac Compatible: Yes, but Macintosh use is not officially supported. Their software should work with Mac OS 8 or later and a Java enabled web browser.
System Requirements: Windows 95 or later. No software download required. Guts Poker works through a web browser using Java scripts. Must have Internet Explorer 5 or later, or Netscape 4.x or later. The web browser must be Java enabled. The minimum system is a 266 MHz Pentium with 32 MB RAM. A Pentium III processor with 128 MB RAM is recommended.

Paradise Poker is one of the busiest online poker rooms on the Internet. On average there are about 1500 players competing on 165 tables at any point in time. It is also one of the older and more established online poker rooms.

URL: http://www.paradisepoker.com

Games Offered: Fixed-limit Texas Hold'em, Seven-Card Stud, Five-Card Stud, Five-Card Draw, Seven-Card Stud High/Low Eight or Better, Omaha, Omaha High/Low Eight or Better, Pineapple; Pot-limit and No-Limit Texas Hold'em, Omaha, Omaha High/Low Eight or Better.

Betting Limits: Range from $0.50/$1 up to $20/40.

Promotions: Check their Promotions page for current offerings. Past promotions have included sign-up bonuses and bad beat jackpots.

Tournaments: Everyday, 24 hours per day, for all of the above games. Buy-ins range from $5 to $100 depending on the table. These are single table tournaments that take about one hour.

Mac Compatible: No.

System Requirements: Must download software from the site in order to play. Need Windows 95 or later with at least a 100 MHz Pentium processor, 32 MB of RAM and 6 MB hard drive storage.

Party Poker is a recent but fast growing playing venue hosted by poker professional Mike Sexton. They began hosting an annual $1 million poker tournament aboard a cruise ship in March, 2002. It is possible for players to qualify for their $1 million event, by winning online tournaments that have $25 buy-ins.

URL: http://www.partypoker.com

Games Offered: Fixed-limit Texas Hold'em, Seven-Card Stud, Seven-Card Stud High/Low Eight or Better, Omaha, Omaha High/Low Eight or Better; Pot-limit and No-Limit Texas Hold'em, Omaha; Pot-limit Omaha High/Low Eight or Better.

Betting Limits: Range from $0.25/$0.50 up to $10/$20.

Promotions: Sign up bonus. Check their News and Events page for additional offerings.

Tournaments: Offers single table tournaments with buy-ins ranging from $5 to $50, and multi-table tournaments with buy-ins ranging from $10 to $100. Check their News and Events page for current tournament offerings and schedules.

Mac Compatible: No

System Requirements: Must download software from the site in order to play. Need Windows 95 or later with at least a Pentium processor, 32 MB of RAM and 3.1 MB available hard drive storage.

Planet Poker was the first cardroom on the Internet and celebrates their 5th Anniversary in 2003. They offer a wide variety of poker games and betting limits. Endorsing this site is the legendary "Mad Genius of poker" himself, Mike Caro; a poker player and instructor, who offers online tips and advice. Roy Cooke is Planet Poker's cardroom manager. Roy played professional poker for 16 years and is currently the leading columnist for *Card Player* magazine.

URL: http://www.planetpoker.com

Games Offered: Fixed-limit Texas Hold'em, Seven-Card Stud, Seven-Card Stud High/Low Eight or Better, Omaha, Omaha High/Low Eight or Better, Razz, Five-Card Draw, Five-Card Draw Low; Pot-limit and No-Limit Texas Hold'em, Omaha, and Omaha High/Low Eight or Better.

Betting Limits: Range from $0.05/$0.10 up to $20/$40.

Promotions: $100,000 progressive bad beat jackpots, a referral program and a loyalty program.

Tournaments: Daily scheduled tournaments. Check the Tournament Registration page for current information.

Mac Compatible: No

System Requirements: Must download software from the site. Windows 95 or later and a Pentium processor are required.

Poker Club is one of the Internet's three original poker rooms. Established in 1999, it originally operated under the name Poker.com.

> *URL:* http://www.thepokerclub.com
> *Games Offered:* Fixed-limit Texas Hold'em, Seven-Card Stud, Seven-Card Stud High/Low Eight or Better, Omaha, Omaha High/Low Eight or Better, Five-Card Stud; Pot-limit and No-limit Texas Hold'em.
> *Betting Limits:* Range from $0.50/$1 up to $20/$40.
> *Promotions:* Deposit bonus on intial sign up, frequent player points program, bad beat jackpots.
> *Tournaments:* Single table tournaments that last about one hour are available 24 hours a day, 7 days a week. Buy-ins range from $5 to $100.
> *Mac Compatible:* No
> *System Requirements:* Windows 95 or later. Software download requires 5 MB of hard drive storage. A 120 MHz Pentium processor with 16 MB of RAM needed to run. 800x600 or higher screen resolution.

Poker On TV features software with high-resolution 3-D graphics and "chat boxes" to converse with other players.

> *URL:* http://www.pokerontv.com
> *Games Offered:* Fixed-limit Texas Hold'em, Seven-Card Stud, Five-Card Stud, Omaha, Omaha High/Low Eight or Better.
> *Betting Limits:* Range from $0.50/$1 up to $20/$40.
> *Promotions:* New players receive a sign-up bonus. Check their site for updates.
> *Tournaments:* None available at this writing. Tournaments are planned for the future.
> *Mac Compatible:* No
> *System Requirements:* Windows 95 or later. Software download requires 5 MB of hard drive storage. A 120 MHz Pentium processor with 16 MB of RAM needed to run.

Poker Room only offers Texas Hold'em, but it is one of the few sites that can be used easily from a Macintosh. In fact the site is completely cross platform since it uses the Java programming language and can run from inside any web browser configured to run Java scripts. Check out their statistics page.

> *URL:* http://www.pokerroom.com
> *Games Offered:* Fixed-limit Texas Hold'em
> *Betting Limits:* Range from $1-$2 up to $25-$50.
> *Promotions:* Deposit bonus on initial sign-up. Additional deposit bonuses based on a Player Points System.
> *Tournaments:* Every day at 8 PM Eastern Time that have a $20 buy-in plus $2 fee. Play money tournaments Monday–Friday and Sunday at 3 PM Eastern Time. Winner receives $50 in real money.
> *Mac Compatible:* Yes. Requires installation of Macintosh Runtime for Java (MJR) 2.0 or later.
> *System Requirements:* A web browser that supports Java 1.1 or later. Internet Explorer 5.0 or later and Netscape 4.x or later provide Java support.

Poker Stars offers a variety of special features with their player interface. Software will accumulate statistical data on your play and on request, email a summary to you. The statistical data is intended to help you analyze your betting patterns and is only made available to you, not your opponents. Poker Stars does have a feature that allows you to make and save notes on your opponents for future reference. Again, the notes you make are for your private use.

> *URL:* http://www.pokerstars.com
> *Games Offered:* Fixed-limit Texas Hold'em, Seven-Card Stud, Seven-Card Stud High/Low Eight or Better, Omaha, Omaha High/Low Eight or Better; Pot-limit and No-Limit Texas Hold'em, Omaha, and Omaha High/Low Eight or Better.
> *Betting Limits:* Range from $0.50/$1 up to $20/$40.

Promotions: Current promotions include a "Frequent Player Points" system. Check their Home page for additional news and promotions.

Tournaments: Check their Tournament page for current schedule and details.

Mac Compatible: No.

System Requirements: Must download software from the site in order to play. Need Windows 95 or later with at least a 100 MHz Pentium processor, 32 MB of RAM and 10 MB available hard drive storage.

Popular Poker is a site for those whose native language is not English. Visitors can select one of six languages (English, French, German, Spanish, Italian, Portuguese) to view the home page instructions. English is required for the rest of the site. Unique offerings include a variation of Omaha where players receive five pocket cards and a variation of the traditional Texas Hold'em betting structure called "Big River" Hold'em.

URL: http://www.popularpoker.com

Games Offered: Fixed-limit and Pot-limit Texas Hold'em, Omaha, Omaha High/Low Eight or Better, Five-Card Omaha, Big River Texas Hold'em, No Limit Texas Hold'em.

Betting Limits: Range from $0.25/$0.50 up to $20/$40.

Promotions: Check their Promotion page for current offerings. Promotions include a Loyalty Points Program.

Tournaments: A wide variety of single and multi-table tournaments with buy-ins that vary from $5 to $100. Check their Tournament page for current schedules and details.

Mac Compatible: No.

System Requirements: Must download software from the site in order to play. Need Windows 95 or later with at least a Pentium processor, 64 MB of RAM and 10 MB available hard drive storage.

True Poker has one of the most elaborate interfaces on the Internet, with graphics that are in three dimensions. Players have the ability to choose animated characters to represent themselves at the table.

URL: http://www.truepoker.com
Games Offered: Fixed-limit Texas Hold'em, Omaha, Omaha High/Low Eight or Better.
Betting Limits: Range from $1/$2 up to $15/$30.
Promotions: Check their Promotion page for current offerings. Past promotions have included drawings for free trips to Las Vegas, and free invitational tournaments for the most active players.
Tournaments: They offer a variety of daily tournaments that vary in size from 30 to 300 players, and buy-ins that vary from $1 to $60. Check their tournament page for current schedules and details.
Mac Compatible: No.
System Requirements: Must download software from the site in order to play. Need Windows 95 or later with at least a 300 MHz Pentium II processor, 32 MB of RAM and 30 MB available hard drive storage.

Ultimate Bet has some of the more unusual variations of Hold'em such as Pineapple (see Appendix I) Double-Flop Hold'em, Half Pot-Limit Hold'em and MiniBlind® Hold'em (read the explanations of all these variations on their web site). Future plans include an improved Community page where poker players can share experiences and information.

URL: http://www.ultimatebet.com
Games Offered: Fixed-limit Texas Hold'em, Seven-Card Stud, Seven-Card Stud High/Low Eight or Better, Omaha, Omaha High/Low Eight or Better, Pineapple, Pineapple High/Low Eight or Better, Double-Flop Hold'em, MiniBlind Hold'em; Half Pot-Limit, Pot-Limit, and No-Limit Texas Hold'em.

Betting Limits: Range from $0.25/$0.50 up to $50/$100.

Promotions: Include High Hand Jackpots and a Player Rewards Club that allows members to earn points redeemable for travel and merchandise.

Tournaments: Check their News and Promotions page for monthly tournament offerings. The Ultimate Contests page describes their regular tournaments.

Mac Compatible: Not directly, but they do provide support for VirtualPC. (See the note to Mac users at the beginning of this section.)

System Requirements: Must download software from the site in order to play. Need Windows 95 or later and a Pentium Processor.

World Poker Room offers the experience of heads up, 1-on-1 Texas Hold'em. Only two players are allowed at the 1-on-1 tables, the button posts the small blind and is the first to act before the flop.

URL: http://www.worldpokerroom.com

Games Offered: Fixed-limit Texas Hold'em, Seven-Card Stud, Five-Card Stud, Omaha, Omaha High/Low Eight or Better.

Betting Limits: Range from $0.25/$0.50 up to $20/$40.

Promotions: Sign up bonus, daily high hand bonus.

Tournaments: Single table Hold'em tournaments available 24 hours per day, 7 days per week. Buy-ins range from $5 to $100. No re-buys allowed. Each tournament lasts about an hour.

Mac Compatible: No

System Requirements: Windows 95 or later. Software download requires 5 MB of hard drive storage. A 120 MHz Pentium processor with 16 MB of RAM needed to run.

World Sports Exchange operates an online sports book and hosts online poker. The site is known for offering private high-limit games (up to $200/$400) on request.

> *URL:* http://www.wsex.com
> *Games Offered:* Fixed-limit Texas Hold'em, Seven-Card Stud, Seven-Card Stud High/Low Eight or Better, Omaha, Omaha High/Low Eight or Better, Five-Card Stud.
> *Betting Limits:* Range from $0.50/$1 up to $30/$60.
> *Promotions:* Check their Promotions page for current and up-coming events. Some of the poker promotions are tied to up-coming sports events.
> *Tournaments:* Single table Hold'em tournaments available 24 hours per day, 7 days per week. Buy-ins range from $5 to $100. No re-buys allowed. Each tournament lasts about an hour.
> *Mac Compatible:* No.
> *System Requirements:* Must download software from the site in order to play. Need Windows 95 or later with at least a 120 MHz Pentium processor, 16 MB of RAM and 4 MB available hard drive storage.

Public Cardrooms

The following is a directory of 220 cardrooms throughout the United States and Canada that offer Texas Hold'em poker. The information, current as of January, 2003, includes addresses, phone numbers, and when available, Web sites. For updated information and additional links to Web sites, go to the companion Web site for this book— http://www.intelligentpoker.com.

There are hundreds of cardrooms scattered throughout the United States because most states have some form of legalized gambling. However, not all casinos have a cardroom and not all cardrooms offer Texas Hold'em. The operation of cardrooms and the games available are subject to change. The listings in this book are not meant to be all-inclusive. Before planning a trip to any cardroom, call ahead and inquire about the hours of operation, games available, the structure of the games, the betting limits, and the current house rules. Most of the cardrooms listed below offer regularly scheduled poker tournaments. Call to inquire about tournament schedules, buy-ins, and prizes.

The cardrooms listed for the United States are sorted by state and grouped into regions. Nearly half of the 197 United States listings are located in Nevada and California. The U. S. regions are:
- Southern Nevada (29 listings)
- Northern Nevada (11 listings)
- Southern California (22 listings)
- Central California (5 listings)
- Northern California (26 listings)
- Pacific Northwest (26 listings for Oregon and Washington)
- Southwest (19 listings for Arizona, New Mexico, and Texas)
- West (9 listings for Colorada and Montana)
- North (9 listings for Minnesota and South Dakota)
- Central (10 listings for Iowa, Kansas, and Missouri)
- Midwest (7 listings for Indiana and Michigan)
- South (15 listings for Louisiana and Mississippi)
- Northeast (9 listings for Connecticut, New Jersey, and New York)

Southern Nevada

Arizona Charlies Hotel & Casino
740 South Decatur Blvd.
Las Vegas, NV 89107
702-258-5200
Toll-Free: 1-800-882-5445
http://www.arizonacharlies.com

Bellagio
3600 Las Vegas Blvd. South
Las Vegas, NV 89109
702-693-7291
Toll-Free: 1-888-987-6667
http://www.bellagiolasvegas.com

Binions Horseshoe Casino
128 East Fremont
Las Vegas, NV 89101
702-382-1600
Toll-Free: 1-800-622-6468
http://www.binions.com

Boulder Station
4111 Boulder Highway
Las Vegas, NV 89121
702-432-7577
Toll-Free: 1-800-683-7777
http://www.boulderstation.com

Buffalo Bills
Interstate 15
Primm, NV 89193
702-382-1212
Toll-Free: 1-800-386-7867

CircusCircus
2880 Las Vegas Blvd. South
Las Vegas, NV 89109
702-734-0410
Toll-Free: 1-800-634-3450
http://www.circuscircus.com

Colorado Belle Hotel & Casino
2100 South Casino Drive
Laughlin, NV 89029
702-298-4000
Toll-Free: 1-800-647-6537
http://www.coloradobelle.com

Don Laughlin's Riverside Resort & Casino
1650 Casino Drive
Laughlin, NV 89029
702-298-2535
Toll-Free: 1-800-227-3849
http://www.riversideresort.com

El Cortez
600 Freemont Street
Las Vegas, NV 89101
702-385-5200
Toll-Free: 1-800-634-6703

Excalibur Hotel & Casino
3850 Las Vegas Blvd. South
Las Vegas, NV 89119
702-879-1379
Toll-Free: 1-800-937-7777
http://www.excaliburlasvegas.com

Flamingo Hilton Laughlin
1900 South Casino Drive
Laughlin, NV 89029
702-298-5055
Toll-Free: 1-888-662-LUCK
http://www.laughlinflamingo.com

Luxor Hotel & Casino
3900 Las Vegas Blvd. South
Las Vegas, NV 89119
702-262-4000
Toll-Free: 1-888-777-0188

Mandalay Bay Resort & Casino
3950 Las Vegas Blvd.
Las Vegas, NV 89119
Toll-Free: 1-877-632-7000
http://www.mandalaybay.com

Mirage
3400 Las Vegas Blvd. South
Las Vegas, NV 89109
702-791-7291
Toll-Free: 1-800-374-9000
http://www.themirage.com

Monte Carlo Resort & Casino
3770 Las Vegas Blvd.
Las Vegas, NV 89109
702-730-7777
Toll-Free: 1-800-311-8999
http://www.monte-carlo.com

New Town Tavern
600 West Jackson
Las Vegas, NV 89101
702-647-3995

Oasis Resort Casino Golf Spa
897 West Mesquite Blvd.
Mesquite, NV 89027
702-346-5232
Toll-Free: 1-800-621-0187

Orleans Hotel & Casino
4500 West Tropicana Ave.
Las Vegas, NV 89103
702-365-7150
Toll-Free: 1-800-675-3267

Palace Station
2411 West Sahara Ave.
Las Vegas, NV 89102
702-367-2411
Toll-Free: 1-800-544-2411
http://www.palacestation.com

Palms
4321 West Flamingo Road
Las Vegas, NV 89103
702-942-7777
Toll-Free: 1-866-942-7777
http://www.thepalmslasvegas.com

Plaza Hotel & Casino
One Main Street
Las Vegas, NV 89101
702-386-2249
Toll-Free: 1-800-634-6575
http://www.plazahotelcasino.com

Poker Palace
2757 Las Vegas Blvd. North
North Las Vegas, NV 89030
702-649-3799

River Palms Casino
2700 South Casino Drive
Laughlin, NV 89028
702-298-2139
Toll-Free: 1-800-835-7904
http://www.river-palms.com

Riviera Hotel & Casino
2901 Las Vegas Blvd. South
Las Vegas, NV 89109
702-794-9255
Toll-Free: 1-800-634-6753
http://www.theriviera.com

Sahara Casino
2535 Las Vegas Blvd. South
Las Vegas, NV 89109
702-737-2317
Toll-Free: 1-800-634-6645
http://www.saharavegas.com

Sam's Town
5111 Boulder Highway
Las Vegas, NV 89121
702-456-7777
Toll-Free: 1-800-897-8696
http://www.samstownlv.com

Stardust Resort & Casino
3006 Las Vegas Blvd. South
Las Vegas, NV 89109
702-732-6513
Toll-Free: 1-800-824-6033
http://www.stardustlv.com

Sunset Station
1301 West Sunset Road
Henderson, NV 89014
702-547-7777
Toll-Free: 1-888-SUNSET9

Texas Station Gambling Hall & Hotel
2101 Texas Star Lane
Las Vegas, NV 89130
702-631-1000
Toll-Free: 1-800-654-8888
http://www.texasstation.com

Northern Nevada

Atlantis Casino
3800 South Virginia Street
Reno, NV 89502
775-954-4142
Toll-Free: 1-800-723-6500
http://www.atlantiscasinoresort.com

Ascuaga's Nugget
1100 Nugget Ave.
Sparks, NV 89431
775-356-3300
Toll-Free: 1-800-648-1177
http://www.janugget.com

Boomtown Hotel & Casino
I -80 West
Verdi, NV 89439
775-345-6000
Toll-Free: 1-800-648-3790

Cactus Pete's
1385 Highway 93
Jackpot, NV 89825
775-755-2321
Toll-Free: 1-800-821-1103
http://www.cactuspetes.com

Circus Circus Hotel and Casino
500 North Sierrra Street
Reno, NV 89503
775-329-0711
Toll-Free: 1-800-648-5010
http://www.circusreno.com

Club Cal-Neva
38 East Second Street
Reno, NV 89505
775-785-3203
Toll-Free: 1-877-777-7303
http://www.clubcalneva.com

Eldorado Hotel & Casino
345 North Virgina Street
Reno, NV 89505
775-786-5700
Toll-Free: 1-800-777-5325
http://www.eldoradoreno.com

Harvey's Resort Hotel & Casino
Highway 50
Stateline, NV 89449
775-588-2411
Toll-Free: 1-800-427-8397
http://www.harrahs.com/our_casinos/
hlt

Peppermill Hotel and Casino
2720 South Virginia Street
Reno, NV 89502
775-826-2121
Toll-Free: 1-800-648-6992
http://www.peppermillreno.com

Red Lion Casino
2065 Idaho Street
Elko, NV 89801
775-738-2111

Reno Hilton
2500 East 2nd Street
Reno, NV 89595
775-789-2313
Toll-Free: 1-800-443-3105
http://www.renohilton.com

Southern California

Agua Caliente Casino
32-250 Bob Hope Drive
Rancho Mirage, CA 92270
760-321-2000
http://www.hotwatercasino.com

Bicycle Casino
7301 Eastern Ave.
Bell Gardens, CA 90201
562-806-4646
http://www.thebicyclecasino.com

Casino Morongo
49750 Seminole Drive
Cabazon, CA 92239
909-849-3080
Toll-Free: 1-800-252-4499 ext.3610
http://www.casinomorongo.com

Club Caribe Casino
7617 Atlantic Ave.
Cudahy, CA 90201
323-560-5995

Commerce Casino
6131 East Telegraph Road
Commerce, CA 90040
323-721-2100
http://www.commercecasino.com

Crystal Park Casino Hotel
123 East Artesia Blvd.
Compton, CA 90220
310-631-3838
Toll-Free: 1-800-717-1000
http://www.crystalparkcasino.com

Fantasy Springs Casino
84285 Indio Springs Drive
Indio, CA 92203
760-342-5000
Toll-Free: 1-800-827-2946
http://www.fantasyspringsresort.com

Hawaiian Gardens Casino
11871 Carson Street
Hawaiian Gardens, CA 90716
562-860-5887
http://www.hawaiiangardenscasino.net

Hollywood Park Casino
3883 West Century Blvd.
Inglewood, CA 90303
310-330-2800
Toll-Free: 1-800-888-4972
http://www.playhpc.com

Hustler Casino
1000 West Redondo Beach Blvd.
Gardena, CA 90247
310-719-9800
Toll-Free: 1-877-968-9800
http://www.hustlergaming.com

Lake Elsinore Resort
20930 Malaga Road
Lake Elsinore, CA 92520
909-674-5160
Toll-Free: 1-888-448-5253

Lucky Lady Casino
5526 El Cajon Blvd.
San Diego, CA 92115
619-287-6690

Normandie Casino & Showroom
1045 West Rosecrans Ave.
Gardena, CA 90247
310-352-3400
Toll-Free: 1-800-540-8006
http://www.normandiecasino.com

Ocean's Eleven Casino
121 Brooks Street
Oceanside, CA 92054
760-439-6988
Toll-Free: 1-888-439-6988
http://www.oceans11.com

Palomar Card Club
2724 El Cajon Blvd.
San Diego, CA 92104
619-280-5828

Pechanga Entertainment Centre
45000 Pala Road
Temecula, CA 92592
909-693-1819
Toll-Free: 1-888-PECHANGA
http://www.pechanga.com

Player's Club
906 North Ventura Ave.
Ventura, CA 93001
805-643-7009

San Manuel
5797 North Victoria
Highland, CA 92346
909-864-5050
Toll-Free: 1-800-359-2464
http://www.sanmanuel.com

Spa Hotel and Casino
100 North Indian Canyon Drive
Palm Springs, CA 92262
760-323-5865
Toll-Free: 1-800-258-2WIN
http://www.sparesortcasino.com

Spotlight 29
46200 Harrison Place
Coachella, CA 92236
760-775-5566
Toll-Free: 1-800-841-6666

Sycuan Casino
5469 Dehesa Road
El Cajon, CA 92019
619-445-6002
Toll-Free: 1-800-279-2826
http://www.sycuancasino.com

Viejas Casino
5000 Willows Road
Alpine, CA 91901
619-445-5400
Toll-Free: 1-800-847-6537
http://www.viejas.com

Central California

Central Coast Casino
359 Grand Ave.
Grover Beach, CA 93433
805-474-8500
http://www.centralcoastcasino.com

Chumash Casino
3400 East Highway 246
Santa Ynez, CA 93460
805-688-3850
Toll-Free: 1-800-728-9997
http://www.chumashcasino.com

Club One Casino Inc
1033 Van Ness Ave.
Fresno, CA 93721
559-497-3000

Golden West Casino
1001, South Union Ave.
Bakersfield, CA 93307
661-324-6936

Paiute Palace Casino
2742 North Sierra H
Bishop, CA 93514
760-873-4150
Toll-Free: 1-888-3PAIUTE
http://www.paiutepalace.com

Northern California

Angies Poker Club
114, West 15th Street
Chico, CA 95928
530-892-2282

Artichoke Joe's
659 Huntington Ave.
San Bruno, CA 94066
650-589-3145

Bay 101
1801 Bering Drive
San Jose, CA 95112
408-451-8888
http://www.bay101.com

Cache Creek Casino
14455 Highway 16
Brooks, CA 95606
530-796-3118
Toll-Free: 1-800-992-8686
http://www.cachecreek.com

California Grand
5867 Pacheco Blvd.
Pacheco, CA 94553
925-685-8397
http://www.calgrandcasino.com

Cameo Club
5757 Pacific Ave.
Stockton, CA 95207
209-474-1777

Casino Real
1030 B West Yosemite
Manteca, CA 95336
209-239-1455

Casino San Pablo
13255 San Pablo Ave.
San Pablo, CA 94806
510-215-7888
http://www.casino-sanpablo.com

Cher-ae Heights
27 Scenic Drive
Trinidad, CA 95570
707-677-3611
Toll-Free: 1-800-684-2464
http://www.cheraeheightscasino.com

Colusa Casino
3770 Highway 45
Colusa, CA 95932
530-458-8844
http://www.colusacasino.com

Comstock Card Room
125 West 11th Street
Tracey, CA 95376
209-832-1111

Don Juan Casino
2785 Don Juan Road
Rancho Cordova, CA 95670
916-851-1512

Duffy's Card Room & Casino
1944 El Camino Ave.
Sacramento, CA 95815
916-920-5809

Elk Valley Casino
2500 Howland Hills Road
Cresent City, CA 95531
707-464-1020
Toll-Free: 1-888-574-2744
http://www.elkvalleycasino.com

Garden City Casino
360 South Saratoga
San Jose, CA 95129
408-244-3333

Lucky Buck Card Club
1620 Railroad Ave.
Livermore, CA 94550
925-455-6144

Lucky Chances Casino
1700 Hillside Blvd.
Colma, CA 94014
650-758-2237
http://www.luckychances.com

Lucky Derby
7433 Greenback Lane
Citrus Heights, CA 95610
916-726-8946
http://www.lucky-derby.com

Napa Valley Casino
3466 Broadway
American Canyon, CA 94503
707-644-8851

Oakdale Card Room
112 North Yosemite Ave.
Oakdale, CA 95361
209-847-2919

Oaks Card Club
4097 San Pablo Ave.
Emeryville, CA 94608
510-653-4456

Outpost Casino
2251 San Ramon Valley Blvd.
San Ramon, CA 94583
925-837-6606

Palace Card Club
22821 Mission Blvd.
Hayward, CA 94541
510-582-1166
http://www.palacecardclub.com

River Cardrooom
246 Petaluma Blvd. North
Petaluma, CA 94952
707-782-9453

Robinson Rancheria Bingo and Casino
1545 East Highway 20
Nice, CA 95464
707-275-9000
Toll-Free: 1-800-809-3636
http://www.robinsonrancheria.biz

Win River Casino
2100 Redding Rancheria Road.
Redding, CA 96001
530-243-3377
Toll-Free: 1-800-280-UWIN
http://www.win-river.com

Pacific Northwest

Oregon

Chinook Winds Casino
1777 Northwest 44th Street
Lincoln City, OR 97367
541-996-5825
Toll-Free: 1-888-244-6665
http://www.chinookwindscasino.com

Kahneeta High Desert Resort and Casino
6823 Highway 8
Warm Springs, OR 97761
541-553-4895
Toll-Free: 1-800-554-4SUN
http://www.kahneeta.com

Kla-Mo-Ya Casino
34333 Highway 97 North
Chiloquin, OR 97624
541-783-7529
Toll-Free: 1-888-552-6692
http://www.klamoya.com

Seven Feathers Casino
146 Chief Miwaleta Lane
Canyonville, OR 97417
541-839-1111
Toll-Free: 1-800-548-8461
http://www.7feathers.com

Spirit Mountain Casino
27100 Southwest Highway 18
Grand Ronde, OR 97347
503-879-2350
Toll-Free: 1-800-760-7977
http://www.spirit-mountain.com

Wild Horse Casino & Resort
72777 Highway 331
Pendelton, OR 97801
541-278-2274
Toll-Free: 1-800-654-9453
http://www.wildhorseresort.com

Washington

Aces Casino
100001 East Sprague Ave.
Spokane, WA 99206
509-892-5242
http://www.acescasinospokane.com

Bally Motor Inn & Restaurant
3333 Matin Way East
Olympia, WA 98506
360-491-5166

Diamond Lil's Cardroom
321 Rainier Avenue South
Renton, WA 98055
425-255-9037
http://www.freddiesclub.com/lils

Emerald Queen Casino
2102 Alexander Ave.
Tacoma, WA 98421
253-594-7777
Toll-Free: 1-888-831-7655
http://www.emeraldqueen.com

Harry's Place
3529 East McKinley Ave.
Tacoma, WA 98404
253-272-0555

Hi Joy Resaurant & Bowl
1011 Bethel Ave.
Port Orchard, WA 98366
360-876-8111

Hideaway Cardroom
14502 Aurora North
Seattle, WA 98133
206-362-9494

Kenmore Lanes Cardroom
7638 Northeast Bothell Way
Bothell, WA 98011
425-486-8646

Last Frontier
225 West 4th Street
La Center, WA 98629
360-573-6442

Little Creek Casino
West 91 Highway 108
Shelton, WA 98584
360-427-7711
Toll-Free: 1-800-667-7711
http://www.little-creek.com

Mac's Tavern and Cardroom
210 East Heron
Aberdeen, WA 98520
360-533-3932

Magic Lanes Cardroom
10612 15th Avenue Southwest
Seattle, WA 98146
206-244-5060

Muckleshoot Casino
2402 Auburn Way South
Auburn, WA 98002
253-804-4444
Toll-Free: 1-800-804-4944
http://www.muckleshootcasino.com

Northern Quest
100 Hayford Road
Airway Heights, WA 99001
509-242-7000
Toll-Free: 1-888-603-7051
http://www.northernquest.net

Riverbend Casino
2721 North Market Street
Spokane, WA 99207
509-483-9499

Shoalwater casino
4112 Highway 105
Tokeland, WA 98590
360-267-2048
Toll-Free: 1-800-801-3401

Sport Center
214 East Yakima Ave.
Yakima, WA 98901
509-453-3300

Suquamish Clearwater Casino
15347 Suquamish Way Northeast
Suquamish, WA 98392
360-598-6889
Toll-Free: 1-800-375-6073
http://www.clearwatercasino.com

Swinomish Casino
12885 Casino Drive
Anacortes, WA 98221
360-293-2691
Toll-Free: 1-800-375-6073
http://www.swinomishcasino.com

Tulalip Casino & Bingo
6410 33rd Avenue Northeast
Marysville, WA 98271
360-651-1111
Toll-Free: 1-888-272-1111
http://html.tulalipcasino.com

Southwest

Arizona

Apache Gold Casino
Old Highway 70
San Carlos, AZ 85550
520-425-7800
Toll-Free: 1-800-272-2438
http://
www.apachegoldcasinoresort.com

Bucky's Casino
1500 Highway 69
Prescott, AZ 86304
520-541-9482
Toll-Free: 1-800-756-8744
http://www.buckyscasino.com

Casino Arizona at Salt River
101 and McKellips
Scottsdale, AZ 85256
480-850-7923
http://www.casinoaz.com

Cliff Castle Casino
353 Middle Verde Road
Camp Verde, AZ 86322
520-567-7952
Toll-Free: 1-800-381-7568
http://www.cliffcastlecasino.net

Desert Diamond Casino
1100 West Pima Mine Road
Sahuarita, AZ 85629
520-393-2795
Toll-Free: 866-332-9467
http://www.desertdiamondcasino.com

Fort McDowell Casino
10424, Noth Fort McDowell Road
Fountain Hills AZ 85264
480-837-1424
Toll-Free: 1-800-843-3678
http://www.fortmcdowellcasino.com

Gila River Casino at Vee Quiva
6443, Komatke Lane
Laveen, AZ 85339
520-796 7777
Toll-Free: 1-800-946-4452
http://www.wingilariver.com

Harrah's Phoenix AK-Chin Casino
15406, Maricopa Road
Maricopa, AZ 85239
480-802-5000
Toll-Free: 1-800-427-7247
http://www.harrahs.com/our_casinos/
akc

Hon-Dah Casino
777 Highway 260
Pinetop, AZ 85935
928-369-0299
Toll-Free: 1-800-929-8744
http://www.hon-dah.com

Mazatzal Casino
Tonto Apache Reservation
Highway 87
Payson, AZ 85541
520-474-6044
Toll-Free: 1-800-777-PLAY
http://www.777play.com

Quechan Paradise Casino
450 Quechan Drive
Yuma, AZ 85364
760-572-7777
Toll-Free: 1-888-777-4946

New Mexico

Casino Apache
Route 4, Carrizo Canyon Road
Mescalero, NM 88340
505-464-4125
Toll-Free: 1-877-277-5677

Cities of Gold Casino
10-B City of Gold Road
Santa Fe, NM 87501
505-455-3313
Toll-Free: 1-800-455-3313

Isleta Casino and Resort
11000 Broadway SE
Albuquerque, NM 87105
505-724-3874
Toll-Free: 1-800-460-5686
http://www.isletacasinoresort.com

Sandia Casino
30 Rainbow Road Northeast
Albuquerque, NM 87113
505-796-7737
Toll-Free: 1-800-526-9366
http://www.sandiacasino.com

Santa Ana Star Casino
54 Jemez Canyon Dam Road
Bernalillo NM 87004
505-867-0000
http://www.santaanastar.com

Sky City Casino
Exit 102, Highway I-40
San Fidel, NM 87049
505-552-5210
Toll-Free: 1- 888-SKYCITY
http://www.skycitycasino.com

Texas

Lucky Eagle Casino
7777 Lucky Eagle Road
Eagle Pass, TX 78852
830-758-1936
Toll-Free: 1-888-255-8259

Speaking Rock Casino
122 South Old Pueblo Road
El Paso, TX 79907
915-860-7777
Toll-Free: 1-800-772-4646
http://www.speakingrockcasino.com

West

Colorado

**Harvey's Wagon Wheel Hotel &
Casino**
321 Gregory Street
Central City, CO 80427
303-582-0800
Toll-Free: 1-800-924-6646

Midnight Rose Casino
256 East Bennett Ave.
Cripple Creek, CO 80813
719-689-0303
Toll-Free: 1-800-635-5825
http://www.midnightrose.com

Ute Mountain Casino
3 Weeminuche Drive
Towaoc, CO 81334
970-565-8800
Toll-Free: 1-800-258-8007
http://www.utemountaincasino.com

Montana

Cassidy's Poker Room
105 South Main
Plentywood, MT 59254
406-765-1116

Eagle Nest Casino
1515 4th Avenue North
Billings, MT 59101
406-259-1104

Locomotive Inn Casino
216 1st Avenue South
Laurel, MT 59404
406-628-7969

Sawbuck Saloon
1301 South Main
Kalispell, MT 59901
406-755-4778

Shooters Casino
1600 Avenue D
Billings, MT 59105
406-252-6220

Silverstrip Casino
680 SW Higgins Ave.
Missoula, MT 59803
406-728-5643

North

Minnesota

Canterbury Park Card Club
1100 Canturbury Road
Shakopee, MN 55379
(952) 445-7223
Toll-Free: 1-866-667-6537
http://www.canterburypark.com/card/
home.html

Shooting Star Casino and Hotel
777 Casino Road
Mahnomen, MN 56557
218-935-2711
Toll-Free: 1-800-453-STAR
http://www.starcasino.com

South Dakota

Dakota Sioux Casino
16415 Sioux Conifer Road
Watertown, SD 57201
605-882-2051
Toll-Free: 1-800-658-4717
http://www.dakotasioux.com

Fort Randall Casino
RR One
Wagner, SD 57380
605-487-7871
Toll-Free: 1-800-362-6333
http://www.fortrandall.com

Gold Dust
688 Main Street
Deadwood, SD 57732
605-578-2100
Toll-Free: 1-800-456-0533
http://www.golddustgaming.com/

Golden Buffalo Casino & Resort
321 Sitting Bull Lane
Lower Brule, SD 57548
605-473-5577

Grand River Casino
Highway 20
Mobridge, SD 57601
605-845-7104
Toll-Free: 1-800-475-3321
http://www.grandrivercasino.com

Miss Kitty's Casino
647 Main Street
Deadwood, SD 57732
605-578-1811

Old Style Saloon #10
657 Main Street
Deadwood, SD 57732
605-578-3346
Toll-Free: 1-800-952-9398
http://www.saloon10.com

Central

Iowa

Casinomaha
1 Blackbird Bend
Onawa, IA 51040
712-423-3700
Toll-Free: 1-800-858-8238

Catfish Bend Riverboat Casino
902 Riverview Drive
Fort Madison, IA 52627
319-753-2946
http://www.catfishbendcasino.com

Isle of Capri Bettendorf
1821 State Street
Bettendorf, IA 52722
563-344-2693
Toll-Free: 1-800-724-5825
http://www.isleofcapricasino.com/
Bettendorf

Meskwaki Casino
1504 305th Street
Tama, IA 52339
641-484-2108
Toll-Free: 1-800-728-4263
http://www.meskwaki.com

Winnavegas Casino
1500 330th Street
Sloan, IA 51055
712-428-7119
Toll-Free: 1-800-468-9466
http://www.winnavegas-casino.com

Kansas

Golden Eagle Casino
1121 Goldfinch Road
Horton, KS 66439
785-486-6601
Toll-Free: 1-888-464-5825
http://www.goldeneaglecasino.com

Harrah's Prairie Band Casino
12305 150th Road
Mayetta, KS 66509
785-966-7641
Toll-Free: 1-800-HARRAHS
http://www.harrahs.com/our_casinos/
top

Missouri

Ameristar Casino Kansas City
3200 North Station Drive
Kansas City, MO 64161
816-414-7068
Toll-Free: 1-800-499-4961
http://www.ameristarcasinos.com/
kansas_city.asp

Ameristar Casino St. Charles
1260 South Main Street
Saint Charles, MO 63302
636-949-7777
Toll-Free: 1-800-325-7777
http://www.ameristarcasinos.com/
st_charles.asp

President Casino Laclede's Landing
800 North First Street
Saint Louis, MO 63102
314-622-1111
Toll-Free: 1-800-772-3647
http://www.presidentcasino.com/
stlouis

Midwest

Indiana

Caesars Indiana
11999 Avenue of the Emperors
Bridgeport, IN 47117
Toll-Free: 1-888-766-2648
http://www.caesars.com/indiana

Casino Aztar
421 Northwest Riverside Drive
Evansville, IN 47708
812-433-4002
Toll-Free: 1-800-DIALFUN
http://www.casinoaztar.com

Harrah's East Chicago Casino
777 Harrah's Blvd.
East Chicago, IN 46312
219-378-3000
Toll-Free: 877.496.1777
http://www.harrahs.com/our_casinos/ech

Michigan

Chip Inn Island Resort Casino
W399 Highway 2 & 41
Harris, MI 49845
906-466-2941
Toll-Free: 1-800-682-6040
http://www.chipincasino.com

Greektown Casino
555 East Lafayette
Detroit, MI 83241
Toll-Free: 1-888-771-4386
http://www.greektowncasino.net

Kewadin Shores Casino
3039 Mackinac Trail
Saint Ignace, MI 49781
906-643-7071
Toll-Free: 1-800-539-2346
http://www.kewadin.com/kewadin.html

Soaring Eagle Casino
6800 Soaring Eagle Blvd.
Mount Pleasant, MI 48858
517-775-5777
Toll-Free: 1-888-7EAGLE7
http://www.soaringeaglecasino.com

South

Louisiana

Grand Casino Coushatta
77 Coushatta Drive
Kinder, LA 70648
337-378-1370
Toll-Free: 1-800-584-7263
http://www.gccoushatta.com

Harrah's Casino New Orleans
512 South Peters Road
New Orleans, LA 70130
504-533-6000
http://www.harrahs.com/our_casinos/nor

Isle of Capri Casino
307 I-10 Service Road
Lake Charles, LA 70669
318-430-2407
Toll-Free: 1-800-843-4753
http://www.isleofcapricasino.com/Lake_Charles

Treasure Chest Casino
5050 Williams Blvd.
Kenner, LA 70065
504-443-8000
Toll-Free: 1-800-298-0711
http://www.treasurechestcasino.com

Mississippi

Ameristar Casino
4146 Washington Street
Vicksburg, MS 39180
662-638-1000
Toll-Free: 1-800-700-7770
http://www.ameristarcasinos.com/
vicksburg.asp

Bayou Casino
242 S. Walnut Street
Greenville, MS 38701
662-335-1111
Toll-Free: 1-800-946-6673

Gold Strike Casino Resort
1010 Casino Center Drive
Robinsonville, MS 38664
662-357-1111
Toll-Free: 1-888-24K-STAY
http://www.goldstrikemississippi.com

Grand Casino Biloxi
265 Beach Blvd.
Biloxi, MS 39530
228-436-2946
Toll-Free: 1-800-946-2946
http://www.grandbiloxi.com

Grand Casino Gulfport
3215 West Beach Blvd.
Gulfport, MS 39501
228-870-7777
Toll-Free: 1-800-946-7777
http://www.grandgulfport.com

Grand Casino Tunica
13615 Old Highway 61 North
Robinsonville, MS 38664
662-363-2788
Toll-Free: 1-800-946-4946
http://www.grandtunica.com

Hollywood Casino-Tunica
1150 Casino Strip Blvd.
Robinsonville, MS 38664
662-357-7700
Toll-Free: 1-800-871-0711
http://www.hollywoodtunica.com

Horseshoe Casino Hotel
1021 Casino Center Drive
Robinsonville, MS 38664
662-357-5500
Toll-Free: 1-800-303-7463
http://www.horseshoe.com/tunica

President Casino Broadwater Resort
2110 Beach Blvd.
Biloxi, MS 39531
228-388-2211
Toll-Free: 1-800-843-7737
http://www.presidentbroadwater.com

Sam's Town Hotel & Casino
1477 Casino Strip Resort Blvd.
Robinsonville, MS 38664
662-363-0711
Toll-Free: 1-800-456-0711
http://www.samstowntunica.com

Silverstar Resort & Casino
Choctaw Shopping Center
Highway 16 West
Philadelphia, MS 39350
662-656-3400
Toll-Free: 1-800-557-0711
http://www.silverstarresort.com

Northeast

Connecticut

Foxwoods Resort Casino
39 Norwich Westerly Road
Mashantucket, CT 06339
860-312-3000
Toll-Free: 1-800-48-POKER
http://www.foxwoods.com

Mohegan Sun
1 Mohegan Sun Blvd.
Uncasville, CT 06382
860-204-8066
Toll-Free: 1-888-226-7711
http://www.mohegansun.com

New Jersey

Bally's Park Place
Park Place & Boardwalk
Atlantic City, NJ 08401
609-340-2000
Toll-Free: 1-800-772-7777
http://www.ballysac.com

Harrah's Atlantic City
777 Harrahs Blvd.
Atlantic City, NJ 08401
609-441-5741
Toll-Free: 1-800-242-7724
http://www.harrahs.com /our_casinos/
atl

Rounders
140 Baekeland Avenue
Middlesex, NJ 08846
732-271-0003
http://www.roundersnj.com

Tropicana Casino & Resort
Brighton Ave. & The Boardwalk
Atlantic City, NJ 08401
609-340-4000
Toll-Free: 1-800-843-8767
http://www.tropicana.net

Trump Taj Mahal
1000 Boardwalk at Virginia Ave.
Atlantic City, NJ 08401
609-449-1000
Toll-Free: 1-800-72-POKER
http://www.trumptaj.com

New York

Akwesasne Mohawk Casino
Route 37
Hogansburg, NY 13655
518-358-2222
Toll-Free: 1-888-622-1155
http://www.mohawkcasino.com

Turning Stone Casino & Resort
5218 Patrick Road
Verona, NY 13478
315-361-7711
Toll-Free: 1-800-771-7711
http://www.turning-stone.com

Canadian Cardrooms
(23 Listings)

Baccarat Casino
10124 103a Ave.
Edmonton, Alberta
780-413-9102

Cash Casino Alberta
4040 B Blackfoot Trail Southeast
Calgary, Alberta
403-243-2273
http://www.cashcasino.ca

Casino ABS Edmonton
7055 Argyll Road
Edmonton, Alberta
780-463-8181

Casino ABS Lethbridge
1251 3rd Avenue South
Leithbridge, Alberta
403-381-9467

Casino Rama
Highway 12
Orillia, Ontario
705-329-3325
Toll-Free: 1-800-832-7529
http://www.casino-rama.com

Casino Regina
1880 Saskatchewan Drive
Regina, Saskatchewan
306-565-3000
Toll-Free: 1-800-555-3189
http://www.casinoregina.com

Casino Yellowhead
12464 153rd Street
Edmonton, Alberta
780-497-7657
http://www.casinoabs.com

Club Regent
1425 Regent Avenue West
Winnipeg, Manitoba
204-957-2700

Elbow River Inn and Casino
1919 Macleod Terrace Southeast
Calgary, Alberta
403- 206-0252
Toll-Free: 1-800-661-1463
http://www.elbowrivercasino.com

Emerald Casino
Prairieland Exhibition Center
503 Ruth Street West
Saskatoon, Saskatchewan
306-683-8845

Gateway Casino
611 Main Street
Vancouver, British Columbia
604-688-9412
http://www.gatewaycasinos.com

Gold Eagle Casino
11902 Railway Avenue East
North Battleford, Saskatchewan
306-446-3833

Grand Casino
725 Marine Drive
Vancouver, British Columbia
604-321-4402

Great Blue Heron Charity Casino
21777 Island Road
Port Perry, Ontario
905-985-4888
Toll-Free: 1-888-29-HERON
http://www.greatblueheroncasino.com

Great Canadian Casino
709 West Broadway
Vancouver, British Columbia
604-872-5543
http://www.greatcanadiancasino.com/
holidayinn.html

Great Canadian Casino
1133 Hastings
Vancouver, British Columbia
604-682-8415
http://www.greatcanadiancasino.com/
renaissance.html

Great Canadian Casino
8440 Bridgeport
Richmond, British Columbia
604-273-1895
http://www.greatcanadiancasino.com/
richmond.html

Lake City Casino
540 Victoria
Kamloops, British Columbia
250-372-3336
http://www.lakecitycasinos.com/
kamloops.php

Lake City Casino
1300 Water Street
Kelowna, British Columbia
250-860-9467
http://www.lakecitycasinos.com/
kelowna.php

McPhillips Street Station Casino
484 McPhillips Street
Winnipeg, Manitoba
204-957-3900
http://www.mlc.mb.ca/mss/
mss_index.htm

Northern Lights Casino
44 Marquis Road
West Prince Albert, Saskatchewan
306-764-4777
http://siga.sk.ca/Northern%20Lights/
northern.htm

Painted Hand Casino
30 3rd Ave.
North Yorkton, Saskatchewan
306-786-6777
http://www.siga.sk.ca/
Painted%20Hand/painted.htm

Palace Casino
2710-8770 170th St.
Edmonton, Alberta
780-444-2112
http://www.palacecasino.com

Appendix I

Hold'em Variations

There are a number of variations of Texas Hold'em, commonly dealt in public cardrooms and over the Internet. Like Hold'em, the variants are structured in a similar way with players receiving pocket cards followed by a flop, and two additional community cards.

Omaha

The most common variation of Hold'em is Omaha, which is played and structured in a similar fashion to Hold'em, but with some key differences. Each player receives *four* pocket cards; there is a round of betting, followed by a 3-card flop, another round of betting, then fourth and fifth community cards, each followed by a round of betting. At showdown each player *must* use two and *only* two of their pocket cards, with three cards from the board to form their hand. It is the requirement that a player use two pockets cards that confuses people familiar with Hold'em. (In Hold'em, your hand can use two, one or none of your pocket cards.)

To see the new consequences of the two pocket-card rule, imagine that your initial hand consisted of all four Aces. Should you bet and see the flop? No, four Aces is a terrible starting hand and should be folded. Only two of those Aces are playable—the other two are dead and will never appear on the board to improve your hand. Reading the board in Omaha is especially challenging because you need to figure out which two of your four pocket cards to play. Imagine holding: K♦, K♥, 5♦, 7♥, and the board has K♣, 4♠, A♥, 8♥, 6♠. What is your hand? At first glance, you might think trip-Kings, but if you consider all the possibilities, you should see that your 5 and 7 completes an 8-high straight.

Pocket Cards:

The Board:

The high hand is an 8-high straight.

Now consider holding 8♥, 9♦, 10♦, J♠ and the board has 6♠, 7♥, Q♥, J♥, 4♥. You will be staring a long time before figuring out that all you have is a pair of Jacks. You cannot complete the straight because you can *only use* two of your cards: You cannot complete the flush because you *must use* two of your cards.

Pocket Cards:

The Board:

The high hand is a pair of Jacks.

In fact, any time the board shows four or five to a flush or straight, you cannot make the hand with just one pocket card. For example, you hold A♠, 9♠, 5♦, 6♠, and the board has 8♥, J♣, Q♥, K♣, 10♠. All you have is a hand with an Ace for a high card. You cannot make any of the straights because you must use two of your cards. By contrast in Texas Hold'em, anyone having a single Ace or 9 would have a straight for this board, because you can use just one of your cards. Their other card wouldn't matter.

Like Hold'em, playing high cards matters most in Omaha, but unlike Hold'em, starting hands are more radically altered by the flop. Your starting hand could be A♣, A♦, K♣, K♦, but if the flop came up 5♥, 4♥, 6♠, you are not the favorite. With four cards in everyone's pocket, someone could easily have two little cards, such as 3, 7 or 7, 8 or a 9, 10 and wait for an 8 to fall, and someone has two Hearts and is drawing to the flush. Your hand cannot make a flush, or a straight, and needs two perfect cards to make a boat. In Hold'em, a flop of little cards such as this probably improved no one and a pair of Aces or a pair of Kings would loom large.

Playing high cards still wins over the long-run in Omaha, but because starting hands can be so radically altered by the flop, fluctuations are larger. If you are at a table with aggressive players, plan on needing a lot of money to stay in the game. Ideally, your starting four cards should all be coordinated; that is, have the potential for a large number of favorable flops. A hand like A♣, K♣, K♦, Q♦, could flop an Ace-high Club flush, a King-high Diamond flush, an Ace-high straight, a King-high straight, a set of Kings, Kings over a smaller pair, or Aces over, if an A,Q fell on the flop. In contrast, a hand such as A♣, 9♦, 8♠, 5♥, is less likely to hit a favorable flop. No flushes are possible with these starting cards and in the unlikely event the flop is 10, J, Q, your straight will probably lose to someone with A, K or K, 10.

It may be tempting to view Omaha as a more complicated game than Hold'em, but ironically, the reverse is true. Omaha is much simpler because with so many cards out, it becomes inevitable that someone will have the nuts. Since the winner usually has the nuts, for you to win, you must have the nuts. Strategy is simple: see the flop as cheaply as possible, and after the flop, unless you have the nuts or a draw to the nuts, fold. Won't this strategy become obvious after a while? Yes, but deviating from it will cost you money. People attracted to Omaha like the excitement of chasing all the drawing possibilities that come up with four pocket cards, and even after they figure out that you always show the nuts, they will still chase you. Unlike Texas Hold'em, where aggression is necessary, it is difficult to play Omaha too tightly. Don't fall into the trap of thinking Hold'em and Omaha are similar games—they are not.

Omaha Eight or Better

This is a variant of Omaha played for a high-low split. It is played exactly like Omaha, only the low hand splits the pot with the high hand. To qualify for a low hand, you cannot have a card higher than an 8. If all hands contain at least one card higher than an 8, the high hand takes the entire pot. Aces can be played low, and often flushes and straights don't count for low. That means the nut low hand would be a wheel A, 2, 3, 4, 5, which could also be a winning high hand (or better yet, a "steel wheel" A, 2, 3, 4, 5, suited).

Obviously, the ideal in such a game is a *scoop* where you take the entire pot by having both the low and high hand. Usually, you are allowed to form two different hands. You use two of your pocket cards to form your high hand, and a different two pocket cards to form your low. Imagine you hold K♣, K♥, 5♦, 4♥, and the board is K♦, 2♣, 3♠, 3♦, 8♥ . For a high hand, you have Kings-full and for a low hand, you have 2♣, 3♠, 4♥, 5♦, 8♥. If you play this game, you will spend most of your time at the table figuring out what you have. Don't be surprised to see pots split three or more ways. Often, two players have identical low hands and are each awarded a quarter of the pot while the winner gets half.

Pocket Cards:

The Board:

The high hand is Kings-full, the low hand is 8-high.

Pineapple

There are many variations of Pineapple, but what they all have in common is that players receive three pocket cards and at some point must discard one. After the discard, which can be before or after the flop, the rules are identical to Texas Hold'em. Since people get to pick their best two pocket cards, winning hands tend to be stronger. This is another game—like Omaha—that should be played tight.

Hold'em variants are especially popular in public cardrooms that have *jackpots*. A jackpot is created by putting a portion of the rake aside into a single pot that grows over the course of time until someone wins it (see Chapter 2). The winner is someone with an unlikely bad beat, like Aces-full losing to four-of-a-kind. Each cardroom has its own definition of what qualifies to win the jackpot. Since bad beats of this nature are rare, jackpots can grow to thousands of dollars before someone wins. However, a monster hand losing to a bigger monster hand is more likely in Hold'em variants than in traditional Hold'em.

When I played in the now defunct Prince George's County Maryland cardrooms, there was bonus money given each day for the first person with Aces-full, Kings-full, etc., high hand for the afternoon, plus $500 for any royal, and $100 for any straight-flush. Under these conditions no one wanted to play anything but Omaha for high, because the higher ranked hands generated by Omaha meant the bonus money was paid out faster.

Appendix II

Poker Tournaments

Poker tournaments have grown in popularity. Hold'em, because it is a faster-paced game than Stud, is a favorite for tournament play. Many of the cardrooms listed in Chapter 10 offer tournaments as well as "live" or "ring" games. A "live" or "ring" game refers to the kind of games described in this book, where all the chips used have a cash value. In a tournament, the chips issued have no cash value, but there are cash prizes at the end for the winners. If you contact a cardroom, inquire about the tournament structures and schedules. Online poker rooms also offer tournaments. Check out the links to online cardrooms also listed in Chapter 10 to see what Internet tournaments are offered. A detailed discussion of tournament play and strategies are beyond the scope of this book, but these events have become so popular, you should know what a poker tournament is.

For poker players, tournaments offer high entertainment value for a fixed dollar amount that is paid up-front. Many tournaments have modest buy-ins (less than $100), which means that for beginners, they offer a low-risk venue for learning the game. The object of the tournament is to determine a winner who will be awarded a cash prize formed from the entry fees. Rarely does one person take all the cash. Usually, there are prizes for the various runner-ups (2nd, 3rd, and so on).

Poker tournaments are analogous in many ways to chess tournaments that for decades have used cash prizes to attract chess players. A chess tournament is easier to understand, so I will first explain the concept of tournament chess. Each entrant in a chess tournament pays an "entry fee." From the pool of money created by the entry fees, a cut goes to the organizers for running the event, but the bulk of the money becomes a prize fund that is awarded to the winners.

The entrants play a series of scheduled and timed chess games. Players who exceed their allotted time to make their moves automatically forfeit their game. After each round of games, the winners are paired against winners so that the number of players with perfect scores reduces by half each time. Usually, the pairing process results in a single perfect score or a small group of people tied with nearly perfect scores who share the prize money.

Poker tournaments are financed in the same way as chess tournaments. The entrants pay a fee up-front that forms the prize fund and pays the organizers. Each entrant is issued a fixed amount of chips to play with that have no cash value. All entrants start play together with the same number of chips. The winner is the person who at the end has accumulated all the chips. The problem becomes how to structure a poker game so that, like a chess tournament, on a timed and scheduled basis, winners are forced to play winners and losers are forced out.

To force losing players out, the betting stakes are continually increased, either at regularly scheduled time intervals or after a specified number of hands. If you don't win chips, the escalating stakes make it more difficult to stay in the game. For example, suppose at the start you are issued $500 of chips and play starts at $5–10. With $500 to start and only $5 blinds to pay, you could sit at the table for many hours without playing a hand. However, in a tournament stakes rise as time passes. Each tournament will have its own schedule for upping the stakes. For example: stakes could start at $5–10, then a half-hour later the stakes could become $10–20, then in another half-hour $20–40, followed by $40–80 and so on. With this kind of doubling, players who sit tight with their chips, or lose them, will eventually be forced all-in just to cover their blinds. As time goes on, only the winners will have enough chips to keep playing. Those forced to go all-in and lose are eliminated from play. Some tournaments do allow "re-buys" in the early stages of play, others do not. If you choose to re-buy, you pay additional money for a second set of chips to continue play.

Obviously, luck has more to do with tournament outcomes than it does the results of ring games. The degree to which luck is a factor depends on how fast the stakes escalate. Imagine an extremely fast schedule where the stakes increase every 10 minutes. Those lucky enough to be dealt winning hands in the first few minutes will have an advantage. But if the scheduled escalation is over a period of hours, the tournament becomes more like live poker with the better players accumulating more chips over the long run.

Because of the time pressure, success at tournament poker requires more aggressive play and a different strategic mindset than live poker. Several books specific to tournament strategies are available. Some recent titles are:

Tournament Poker for Advanced Players, David Sklansky, Two Plus Two Publishing (2002).

Tournament Poker, by Tom McEvoy, Cardsmith Publications (2000).

Poker Tournament Strategies, Sylvester Suzuki. Two Plus Two Publishing (1997).

The Secret to Winning Big in Tournament Poker, Ken Buntjer, Red Rose Publishing (1995).

You can also purchase tournament simulation software such as *Tournament Texas Hold'em for Windows,* by Wilson Software, which is available from ConJelCo—http://www.conjelco.com. Because poker tournaments are structured so differently from live games, practice with a software simulation before actual play is a valuable exercise.

The most famous poker tournament is the annual World Series of Poker, in which anyone willing to pay the $10,000 buy-in can play for the World Championship. The event is held annually in May at Binions Horseshoe Casino in Las Vegas. For more information, go to http://www.binions.com/worldseries.asp. Success at qualifying tournaments is not a requirement, which it usually is for championship tournaments in most other games. The poker variant used to determine the World Champion of Poker is No-Limit Texas Hold'em.

Glossary

all in—when a player places all his or her remaining chips into the pot. Players going all in do not call additional bets, and they cannot compete for additional bets made by other players, which go into a side pot.

bad beat—an improbable loss, such as losing with a very strong hand or losing to someone's long-shot draw.

bet—to place money in the pot that other players must match to remain in the hand.

big blind—the player two seats to the left of the button, who must make a pre-flop bet before receiving pocket cards.

bluffing—betting on a weak hand in order to convince others the hand is strong.

board—the face-up cards on the table (see *community cards*).

boat—alternate term for full house.

button—a small plastic disk used in casino games to mark the player in the "dealer's position." After each hand, the button rotates to the next player on the left. Because a non-playing casino employee deals the cards, the button is moved after each hand, allowing players to takes turns having the advantageous dealer position of acting last.

call—to match another player's bet.

173

cards speak—a rule that players do not have to correctly state the contents of their hand. The dealer will award the pot to the player showing the best cards, regardless of what statements the player made. Casino games are usually played with the *cards speak* rule.

check—to pass on betting.

check-raise—to raise another player's bet after initially checking (see *raise*).

chips—tokens purchased by players for use for placing bets.

community cards—the five cards placed face-up in the center of the table, and used by all the players to form their hands (see *board*).

dealer—the person who deals the cards and manages the money going into the pot. In a casino, the dealer is an employee, not a player in the game.

drawing dead—drawing in a situation where even if the draw is made, the player still loses. For example, if you draw for a flush when someone already has a full-house.

drawing hand—a hand that will not win unless it is improved. Having four cards to a straight or four cards to a flush are examples of drawing hands.

flop—the first three community cards in Hold'em, which are shown all at once.

fold—to drop out of a hand and forfeit all interest in the pot.

free card—seeing a fourth or fifth community card without having to call a bet.

freeroll tournament—a poker tournament with no cash entry fee, but cash prizes for the winners at the end (see *poker tournament*).

high-low split—a poker game where the pot is split by the players holding the highest and lowest hands. In many high-low games, the low hand must qualify to claim half the pot. A common qualification is that the low hand must not have a card higher than an eight. If no low hand qualifies, the high hand takes the entire pot.

implied collusion—a situation where many players are on an improbable draw to beat the best hand.

implied pot odds—the ratio of the total amount of money a player expects to win to the amount of money that a player must contribute to the pot. For example, the pot may contain $50, but you expect five players to call your $10 bet. The implied odds are 10 to 1 since you expect to win $100. Contrast with *pot odds*.

jackpot game—a poker variant found in some casinos where an amount is taken from each pot to accumulate in a jackpot. To win the jackpot, an unlikely poker event must occur. The most common is the "bad beat jackpot" where a player holding Aces-full or higher loses the hand. Jackpots in low-limit Hold'em games can accumulate to tens of thousands of dollars and their existence encourages loser play because players often stay in hands longer than they should in hopes of hitting the jackpot.

kicker—a card that is part of a hand, but not part of a combination. For example, if you hold A, K and the board shows K, 8, 8, 3, Q, your hand is two pair (Kings and eights) with an Ace kicker.

limit Hold'em—a common variation where the bets and raises are limited to fixed amounts in each round of betting. In $5–10 limit Hold'em, bets and raises are in increments $5 before and after the flop and $10 after the turn and river cards.

monster hand—a very high-ranked hand. Aces full, four of a kind, any straight flush, are often referred to as monsters since losses with these kinds of hands are very infrequent.

no-limit Hold'em—a variation where in any betting round, the players can bet any amount up to what they have on the table.

nuts—the highest possible hand that can be formed with the cards on the board.

nut-flush—the highest possible flush that can be formed with the cards on the board.

nut-straight—the highest possible straight that can be formed with the cards on the board.

Omaha—a variation of Hold'em where players receive four pocket cards. A total of five community cards appear on the board, but the players are only allowed to use three of them to form their hand. Players must use two of their four pocket cards to make their hand.

Omaha Eight or Better—a variation of *Omaha* where the high and low hands split the pot. Each player is allowed to form two different hands, one using any two of their pocket cards to make the best possible high, and one using any two of their pocket cards to make the best possible low. To claim the low hand, there can be no card higher than an eight. Straights and flushes do not count in determining low. If no low hand qualifies, the high hand wins the entire pot.

outs—cards that will improve a hand. For example, if you have four to a flush, there are nine outs for making a flush.

overcard—a community card that is higher than either of a player's pocket cards.

Pineapple—a variation of Hold'em where players are dealt three pocket cards, but at some point during the hand, must discard one.

pocket cards—the face-down cards dealt to each player at the beginning of a hand.

poker tournament—an event where players pay an entry fee to form a prize fund. Each participant is issued playing chips that have no cash value. The players who accumulate all the chips during play, win the cash prizes.

position—a player's turn to act in a hand relative to the other players. A player in an early position is one of the first to act; a player in a late position is one of the last. Since late position is an advantage, position rotates one seat after each hand to give players equal turns.

post—a pre-flop bet required when joining a game in progress or when re-entering a game if a turn in the blind position is missed.

pot—the total amount of money wagered on a hand.

pot-limit Hold'em—a variation where in any betting round, the players can bet any amount up to what is currently in the pot.

pot odds—the ratio of the amount of money in the pot to the amount of money that a player must contribute to compete for the pot. For example, if you must call a $10 bet to compete for a $50 pot, the pot odds are 5 to 1.

proposition player—also referred to as a *prop* player, is a person paid by the house to play. The purpose is to have players available to start games or keep a game going. Proposition players play with their own money, so they must be good enough to at least break even at the table, or their pay will not cover their losses.

raise—both matching and increasing a bet made by another player.

rake—a fraction of each pot taken by the casino as a charge for running a poker game.

river card—the fifth and final community card in Hold'em.

royal flush—the highest ranked hand in poker—Ace, King, Queen, Jack, ten, all in the same suit.

scoop—to win the entire pot in a high/low split pot game.

semi-bluffing—betting on a weak hand that has a good chance of improving.

set—three cards of the same rank (also referred to as *trips*).

Seven-Card Stud—a popular poker game where each player receives seven cards and uses five to form their hand. Each player receives three cards initially—two face down and one face-up. The next three cards are dealt face-up and the final card face down. In contrast to Hold'em, there are no shared cards in a Stud game. Players may only use the cards they receive.

showdown—the act of showing cards to determine the winner of a hand.

side pot—a separate pot created after one player goes "all in." Additional money wagered by the players who are not all in goes into the *side pot*. The person going all in cannot compete for the side pot (see *all in*).

slow-play—representing a strong hand as weak by not betting in order to disguise the strength. The opposite of bluffing.

small blind—the person to the immediate left of the person on the button. The small blind is required to place one half a pre-flop bet before receiving their pocket cards. To see the flop, the small blind must later on match the big blind's bet plus any raises (see *big blind*). The small blind has the option of raising.

splashing the pot—throwing chips into the pot in such a way that the dealer is unable to count them. *Splashing the pot* is forbidden in cardroom play.

spread-limit Hold'em—a variation where bets and raises are not in fixed increments but can be any amount up to the specified limit.

string bet—placing a bet, then reaching for more chips in order to raise. *String bets* are forbidden in cardroom play.

table stakes—a rule requiring that all money put in play during a hand must be on the table before the hand begins.

tapped out—losing all the money placed on the table.

tell—a characteristic mannerism or behavior that indicates a player's thinking.

trips—three cards of the same rank (also referred to as *set*).

turn card—the fourth community card in Hold'em.

wheel—a five-high straight: A, 2, 3, 4, 5 of mixed suits.

INDEX

ABOUT THE AUTHOR

Sam Braids has had a life-long fascination with games that combine strategic thinking and psychology. He has spent decades studying and playing poker and chess. He also holds a doctorate in experimental physics and has extensive experience teaching advanced physics and mathematics.

His combined interest in social behavior and mathematics is reflected in his upcoming second book, *Loans, Income, Investments and Other Financial Decisions: Mathematical Deceptions That Cost You Money*. The book will serve as a guide for many kinds of common decisions related to financial planning and expose many widespread deceptive practices employed by financial institutions. He lives near Baltimore, Maryland.

ACKNOWLEDGEMENTS

I wish to thank Arlene Uslander - http://www.theramp.net/auslander, for her careful and enthusiastic editing of the manuscript. I also thank Graham Van Dixhorn of Susan Kendrick Writing, for his thoughtful work writing the back cover and proofreading the book.

Any errors found in this book are mine. Don't hesitate to call errors to my attention or make other comments on this book. I enjoy hearing from my readers. E-mail your feedback to comments@intelligentpoker.com or write the publisher - Intelligent Games Publishing, P. O. Box 6705, Towson, MD 21285.

- Sam Braids